The Blockade Runners

A new translation of the unabridged text with illustrations

JULES VERNE

translated by Karen Loukes
with an introduction and essay by Professor Ian Thompson

Luath Press Limited

EDINBURGH

www.luath.co.uk

First published as *Les Forceurs de blocus*, Paris 1865
First published in English, London 1874
This translation first published 2011

ISBN: 978 1905222 20 9

The publisher acknowledges subsidy from

ALBA | CHRUTHACHAIL

towards the publication of this book

The paper used in this book is recyclable. It is made
from low chlorine pulps produced in a low energy,
low emissions manner from renewable forests.

Printed and bound by
Bell & Bain Ltd., Glasgow

Typeset in 10 point Sabon
by 3btype.com

Background to
The Blockade Runners

WHEN THE AMERICAN CIVIL WAR broke out in April 1861, Jules Verne was 33 years old and his literary career was on the point of taking off. Although at this time he had not yet acquired his own boat, his passion for sailing was already deeply instilled in his creative psyche.

Born and raised in the seaport of Nantes with its connections to the slave trade, Verne was well aware of both transatlantic seafaring and the issues that led up to the Civil War. Moreover, Nantes was a centre of shipbuilding and Verne was fascinated by developments in the technology of marine engineering. This was crystallised in his 1859 journey to Britain, which involved visits to Liverpool and Glasgow, both cities later involved in the provision of blockade runners on behalf of the Confederate States. He was thus ideally qualified to create a novella based on the war, though it must be admitted that issues of marine technology and seamanship, together with a fast moving and romantic plot, predominate to a greater extent than the profound moral issues involved in the war.

Professor Ian Thompson

The Dolphin

THE CLYDE WAS THE first river to have its waters turn to foam under the paddlewheels of a steamer. That was in 1812. The boat was called *The Comet* and provided a regular service between Glasgow and Greenock, travelling at a speed of six nautical miles an hour. Since that time, more than a million steamers or packet boats have travelled up or down the Scottish river, and the inhabitants of the large commercial city must be extremely used to the wonders of steam travel.

Nevertheless, on 3 December 1862, an enormous crowd, made up of ship owners, merchants, factory owners, workers, sailors, women and children, thronged the muddy streets of Glasgow, making for Kelvin Dock, a huge shipbuilding establishment belonging to Messrs Tod and MacGregor. This latter name provides more than ample proof that the famous descendants of the Highlanders have become industrialists and that they have turned all the vassals of the old clans into factory workers.

Kelvin Dock[1] is situated several minutes from the city on the right-hand bank of the Clyde. Its immense yards were soon overrun by inquisitive onlookers; there was no section of quay, no wharf wall, no shop roof that had a vacant space to offer. The river itself was criss-crossed with boats and the heights of Govan on the left-hand bank swarmed with spectators.

The cause of this excitement was not, however, an extraordinary ceremony, but quite simply the launching of a ship. The people of Glasgow could not help but be extremely indifferent about such an operation. So was *The Dolphin* – for such was the name of the vessel constructed by Messrs Tod and MacGregor – in some way special? To be honest, no. She was a large, 1,500-tonne ship made of sheet steel; everything about her had been planned to obtain great speed. Her high-pressure engine came from the work-shops of Lancefield Forge and possessed 500 horsepower. It moved twin screws, situated on either side of the stern-post in the narrow stern and completely independent of one another – an entirely new application of the system invented by Messrs Dudgeon of Millwall, which lends ships great speed and enables them to move in an extremely tight circle. As for *The Dolphin*'s draught, it could hardly be very considerable. The experts were not mistaken when they concluded that this ship was destined to frequent channels of a medium depth. But none of these characteristics justified the public's excitement in any way. In short, *The Dolphin* possessed no more and no less than any other ship. So perhaps its launch presented some mechanical difficulty that had to be over-come? No. The waters of the Clyde had already welcomed many vessels of a more considerable tonnage, and the launching of *The Dolphin* was to be carried out in the most ordinary of ways.

In fact, when the sea was slack and the ebb tide was setting in, operations commenced. Mallet blows rang out in perfect unison, striking the wedges intended to lift the keel of the ship. A shudder soon ran through the whole of her massive structure; although she had been raised only slightly, her shaking could be felt. She began to slide, then to speed up, and, in a few moments, *The Dolphin* left its carefully tallowed slipway and plunged into the Clyde in the midst of thick curls of white steam. Her stern bumped against the muddy riverbed, then she rose on the back of a giant wave, and the magnificent steamer, swept along by her momentum, would have been smashed against the quays of the Govan yards had not all her anchors checked her course, making a formidable noise as they dropped.

Her launch had been a perfect success. *The Dolphin* rocked gently on the waters of the Clyde. All of the spectators clapped their hands when she entered her natural element, and huge cheers arose on both banks.

But why these shouts and this applause? The most passionate of the spectators would doubtless have been at a loss to explain their enthusiasm. So what was behind the very particular interest excited by this ship? Quite simply the mystery surrounding her destination. Nobody knew what type of commerce she was to be used for, and the variety of opinions expressed by the various groups of onlookers on this serious subject was truly astonishing.

However, the best informed, or those who claimed to be such, agreed that this steamer was to play a role in the terrible war that was then decimating the United States of America. But they knew no more, and nobody could say whether *The Dolphin* was a privateer, a transport ship, a Confederate boat or a Federal navy vessel.

'Hurrah!' cried one, maintaining that *The Dolphin* had been built for the use of the Southern States.

'Hip hip hurray!' shouted another, vowing that never would a quicker vessel have cruised along the American coast.

Her purpose was thus unknown, and you would have had to be the partner or at least the intimate friend of Vincent Playfair and Co. of Glasgow to know exactly what it was all about.

The firm that went by the name of Vincent Playfair and Co. was rich, powerful and clever. The old and highly regarded family was descended from the tobacco lords who had built the most beautiful areas of the city. Following the Act of Union, these skilful merchants had founded Glasgow's first trading posts through the trafficking of tobacco from Virginia and Maryland. Immense fortunes were made and a new trading centre was created. Industry and manufacturing quickly established themselves; spinning mills and foundries sprang up on all sides and the city reached the height of its prosperity in several years.

The Playfair firm remained true to the enterprising spirit of its ancestors. The company entered into the most audacious of operations and upheld the honour of Scottish[2] commerce. Its current head Vincent Playfair, a man of 50 with an essentially practical and positive, though daring, nature, was a thoroughbred ship owner. Nothing affected him outside commercial matters, not even the political side of transactions. Yet he was perfectly honest and loyal.

He could not, however, claim responsibility for the idea of constructing and fitting out *The Dolphin*. This belonged exclusively to his nephew James Playfair, a handsome young man of 30 and the boldest skipper in the United Kingdom's merchant navy.

It was in the Tontine Coffee Room beneath the arches of the town hall that James Playfair, after reading the American newspapers with fury, had one day informed his uncle of a very risky venture.

'Uncle Vincent,' he said abruptly, 'we could earn two million in less than one month!'

'What's at stake?' asked Uncle Vincent.

'A ship and her cargo.'

'Nothing else?'

'Yes, the lives of the crew and the captain, but that doesn't count.'

'Let's see,' replied Uncle Vincent.

'You have seen,' resumed James Playfair. 'You've read the *Tribune*, the *New York Herald*, *The Times*, the *Richmond Enquirer* and *The American Review*?'

'Scores of times, nephew.'

'Like me, you think that the war in the United States will last for a long time yet?'

'A very long time.'

'You know how much impact this fight is having on Scotland's interests, especially those of Glasgow?'

'And more specifically those of Playfair and Co.,' replied Uncle Vincent.

'Particularly those,' responded the young captain.

'I grieve about it every day, James, and I cannot but envisage with dread the commercial disasters that this war may bring about. Not that the firm of Playfair isn't solid, but it has contacts that may fail. Ah, those Americans! Be they proslavery or abolitionists, I commend them all to the devil!'

Though humanity's lofty principles, superior to personal interests at all times and in all places, may suggest that

Vincent Playfair was wrong to speak like this, he was right only to consider a purely commercial point of view. The most important American export was in short supply on the Glasgow market. The cotton famine, to use the powerful English expression, was becoming more ominous day by day. Thousands of workers were finding themselves reduced to living off public charity. Glasgow has twenty-five thousand power looms which, before the war in the United States, produced six hundred and twenty-five thousand metres of spun cotton per day, or in other words fifty million pounds per year. The disruption caused to the city's industrial activity when the textile material failed to arrive almost in its entirety can be judged by these figures. Companies collapsed by the hour. Work was suspended in all factories. The workers were dying of hunger.

It was the sight of this extreme poverty that had given James Playfair the idea for his daring venture.

'I will go looking for cotton,' he said, 'and I will bring some back no matter what.'

But as he was as much a man of business as Uncle Vincent, he had resolved to proceed via trade and to propose the operation as a commercial affair.

'Uncle Vincent,' he said, 'here's my idea.'

'Tell me, James.'

'It's very simple. We will construct a ship of great speed and huge capacity.'

'That is possible.'

'We will load it with munitions of war, provisions and clothing.'

'That may well be.'

'I will take command of this steamer. I will challenge all

of the ships of the Federal navy. I will run the blockade of one of the Southern ports.'

'You will sell the cargo to the Confederates who need it at a high price,' said his uncle.

'And I will return with a load of cotton...'

'That they will give to you for nothing.'

'Precisely, Uncle Vincent. How does that sound?'

'Good. But will you get through?'

'I will if I have a good ship.'

'We will make you one specially. But what about the crew?'

'Oh, I will find one. I don't need many men. Enough to manoeuvre, that's all. It isn't a question of fighting the Federals, but of outstripping them.'

'You will outstrip them,' replied Uncle Vincent in a peremptory manner. 'Now tell me, James, which part of the American coast are you planning to make for?'

'Several ships have already run the blockades of New Orleans, Willmington and Savannah, uncle. I am thinking of entering directly at Charleston. No British vessel has yet been able to penetrate these channels except *The Bermuda*. I will do as she did, and if my ship draws little water I will go where the Federal vessels are unable to follow me.'

'The fact is,' said Uncle Vincent, 'that Charleston abounds in cotton. They burn it to be rid of it.'

'Yes,' replied James. 'What's more, the city is almost surrounded. Beauregard is short of munitions; he will pay me a fortune for my cargo.'

'Indeed, nephew! And when do you want to leave?'

'In six months. I will need long winter nights to make it through more easily.'

'We will manage it, nephew.'

'So that's settled, uncle.'

'That's settled.'

'Not a word?'

'Not a word!'

And that is how, five months later, the steamer *The Dolphin* was launched from the Kelvin Dock shipyards and why nobody knew its real destination.

2

Getting Underway

THE DOLPHIN WAS FITTED out quickly. Her rigging was ready and all that remained were final adjustments. *The Dolphin* had three schooner masts – an almost pointless luxury. After all, the ship was not to rely on the wind to escape the Federal cruisers, but on the powerful engine contained within her flanks. And with good reason.

Towards the end of December, *The Dolphin* underwent trials in the Firth of Clyde. It was impossible to say who was more satisfied – the builder or the captain. The new steamer went marvellously and the patent log[3] registered a speed of 17 nautical miles[4] an hour, a speed that no British, French or American ship had ever reached. In a battle with the quickest vessels, *The Dolphin* would most certainly have won a maritime match by several lengths.

Loading commenced on 25 December. The steamer moored at the steamboat quay a little beneath Glasgow Bridge, the last bridge to span the Clyde before its mouth. Vast wharfs contained an immense supply of clothing, weapons and munitions that were quickly transferred into *The Dolphin*'s hold. The nature of this cargo gave away the ship's mysterious destination, and the Playfairs were unable to keep their secret any longer. Moreover, *The Dolphin* was soon to take to the sea. No American cruiser had been reported in British waters. And besides, how could they remain silent for long when it came to forming a crew? It was impossible to take men on board without telling them of their destination. After all, they were going to risk their lives, and when people are going to risk their lives, they like to know how and why.

However, this prospect deterred nobody. Wages were good and everybody had a role in the operation. Thus it was that a large number of the very best sailors appeared, and James Playfair was spoilt for choice. But he chose well, and 24 hours later the muster roll bore the names of 30 sailors who would have done credit to Her Most Gracious Majesty's yacht.

Departure was fixed for 3 January. On 31 December The Dolphin was ready. Her hold abounded with munitions and supplies, her bunkers with coal. There was nothing holding her back.

On 2 January the skipper was on board, taking a final look at his boat, when a man appeared at The Dolphin's gangway and asked to speak to James Playfair. One of the sailors led him onto the poop deck.

He was a strapping fellow with broad shoulders and a florid face, and his simple air failed to hide a certain underlying refinement and gaiety. He did not appear to be familiar with maritime customs and looked around him like a man who was little used to frequenting the deck of a ship. However, he assumed the manners of an old seadog, looking at The Dolphin's rigging and waddling in the way that sailors do.

When he arrived in the captain's presence, he looked at him fixedly and said:

'Captain James Playfair?'

'That's me,' replied the skipper

'That's me,' replied the skipper. 'What do you want?'

'I want you to take me on board.'

'There's no space left. The crew is complete.'

'Oh, one more man won't hinder you. Quite the opposite.'

'Do you think so?' said James Playfair, looking his opposite number straight in the eye.

'I'm sure of it,' replied the sailor.

'But who are you?' asked the captain.

'A rugged sailor, a sturdy fellow and a determined chap, I give you my word. I can offer you two strong arms, which are not to be sniffed at on a ship.'

'But there are vessels other than *The Dolphin* and captains other than James Playfair. Why come here?'

'Because I want to serve on board *The Dolphin* and take orders from Captain James Playfair.'

'I don't need you.'

'A strong man is always needed. If you want me to prove my strength by trying me against three or four of the sturdiest fellows in your crew, I'm ready to do so!'

'That's going a bit far!' replied James Playfair. 'And what's your name?'

'Crockston at your service.'

The captain took several steps back to enable him to better examine this Herculean man who introduced himself in such a forthright manner. The sailor's bearing, size and appearance did not contradict his claim to strength. You could sense that he must be of uncommon force and that he was not lacking in courage.

'Where have you sailed?' Playfair asked him.

'Just about everywhere.'

'And you know what *The Dolphin* is going to do over there?'

'Yes, and that's what attracts me.'

'Well God damn me if I let a fellow of your calibre escape! Go and find the first mate, Mr Mathew, and have your name taken.'

After pronouncing these words, James Playfair expected to see the man turn on his heels and head for the bow of the ship. But he was mistaken; Crockston did not move.

'Well, did you hear me?' the captain asked.

'Yes,' the sailor replied. 'But that's not all. I have something else to propose.'

'You're starting to irritate me,' James responded bluntly. 'I don't have time to waste in conversations.'

'I won't trouble you for long,' Crockston resumed. 'Just a few more words, that's all. I'll tell you what it's about. I have a nephew.'

'He has a fine uncle, this nephew,' replied James Playfair.

'Ha ha!' said Crockston.

'Will you finish?' the captain asked impatiently.

'Well, here's the thing. When you take the uncle, you put up with the nephew as well.'

'Oh, really!'

'Yes, it's customary. One doesn't go without the other.'

'And who exactly is your nephew?'

'A boy of 15, a novice who I'm training. He's very willing and will make a fine sailor one day.'

'Master Crockston,' cried James Playfair, 'do you take *The Dolphin* for a school for ship's boys?'

'Don't speak ill of ship's boys,' retorted the sailor. 'One of them became Admiral Nelson and another Admiral Franklin.'

'By Jove!' replied James Playfair. 'You have a way of speaking that I like. Bring your nephew along. But if I find that his uncle isn't the sturdy fellow that he professes to be, his uncle will have to answer to me. Go, and come back within an hour.'

Crockston did not need to be told twice. He saluted *The Dolphin*'s captain rather clumsily and returned to the quay. An hour later he was back on board with his nephew, a somewhat frail and puny boy of 14 or 15 with a timid, surprised air who did not appear to have inherited his uncle's self-assurance or strong physical qualities. Crockston himself was obliged to urge him on with a few good words of encouragement.

'Let's go,' he said, 'come on! Confound it! Nobody's going to eat us! Anyway, there's still time to leave.'

'No, no!' replied the young man. 'And may God protect us.'

That very day, the names of the sailor Crockston and the novice John Stiggs were entered on *The Dolphin*'s muster roll.

Next morning, at five o'clock, the steamer's fires were stoked up, the deck shook under the vibrations of the boiler, and steam whistled through valves. The hour of departure had arrived.

Despite the early hour, a fairly large crowd was squee-zed onto the quays and onto Glasgow Bridge. They had come to salute the audacious steamer one last time. Vincent Playfair was there to embrace the captain, but he conducted himself on this occasion like an old Roman from the good old days. He maintained a heroic countenance, and the two heartfelt kisses that he favoured his nephew with were the sign of a strong character.

'Go James,' he said to the young captain, 'go quickly and return even more quickly. Above all, don't forget to take advantage of your position. Sell dear, buy cheap and you will have your uncle's esteem.'

With this recommendation, borrowed from the *Manual of the Perfect Merchant*[5], uncle and nephew parted and all the visitors left the ship.

At that moment, Crockston, who was standing next to John Stiggs on the forecastle, said to the latter:

'All's well, all's well! We'll be on the open sea before two o'clock and I have a good feeling about a voyage that starts like this!'

By way of response, the novice squeezed Crockston's hand.

James Playfair then issued his final orders for departure.

'Are we at pressure?' he asked his first mate.

'Yes, captain,' replied Mr Mathew.

'Then cast off the lines.'

The manoeuvre was executed immediately and the screws began to move. *The Dolphin* set off, passed between the ships in the port and quickly disappeared out of sight of the crowd who hailed her with their last hurrahs.

The descent of the Clyde was easily accomplished. It might be said that this river was made by the hand of man, and even by the hand of a master. Thanks to dredges and incessant clearing, it has gained 15 feet in depth over 60 years, and its width has been trebled between the city's quays. The forest of masts and chimneys was soon lost in the smoke and fog. The noise of the foundry hammers and of the hatchets of the building yards faded into the distance. Level with the village of Partick, the factories were replaced with cottages, villas and country houses. *The Dolphin*, moderating

The Dolphin quickly disappeared

the energy of her steam, sailed between the dykes that confine the river above the level of its natural banks and often in the midst of very narrow channels. This is a minor inconvenience, as depth is more important than width for navigable rivers. The steamer, guided by one of those excellent pilots from the Irish Sea, made its way without hesitation between the floating buoys, stone columns and *biggings*[6] surmounted with lanterns that mark the channel. She soon passed Renfrew Castle. The Clyde became broader at the foot of the Kilpatrick Hills and before Bowling Bay, at the end of which opens the mouth of the canal that links Edinburgh with Glasgow.

Finally, the somewhat blurred silhouette of Dumbarton Castle rose up 400 feet in the mist and soon, on the left-hand bank, the ships of Port Glasgow bobbed up and down in *The Dolphin*'s waves. Several miles later, *The Dolphin* passed Greenock, the home town of James Watt. She then found herself at the mouth of the Clyde and at the entrance to the firth that connects the river to the North Channel. There she felt the first undulations of the sea and sailed along the picturesque coast of the Isle of Arran.

Finally, she rounded the promontory of the Mull of Kintyre, which juts out into the channel, and the crew recognised Rathlin Island. The pilot made his way back in his launch to his small cutter which was cruising on the open sea. *The Dolphin*, back in her captain's command, passed around the north of Ireland on a route little frequented by ships and soon, having passed out of sight of the last European land, found herself alone in the open ocean.

3

At Sea

THE DOLPHIN HAD A GOOD crew made up not of men trained for combat and boarding parties, but of skilled sailors. That was all she needed. They were all determined fellows, but were also men of business to a greater or lesser extent. They went in search of a fortune, not glory. They had no flag to fly, no colours to back up with cannon fire. Moreover, the artillery on board consisted of two small cannons suitable only for sending signals.

The Dolphin made rapid progress. She lived up to the hopes of her builders and captain, and soon passed out of British waters. There was not a single ship in sight; the ocean highway was clear. Besides, no Federal navy vessel had the right to attack her under the British flag. They could follow her and prevent her from running the line of the blockade, but no more. Consequently, James Playfair had sacrificed everything in favour of his ship's speed to ensure they were not followed.

Be that as it may, they kept a close watch on board. Despite the cold, there was always a man stationed in the masts, ready to report any sails on the horizon. When evening arrived, James gave Mr Mathew very precise instructions.

'Don't leave your look-outs in the spars for too long,' he

said to him. 'The cold may take hold and men don't keep a close watch in such conditions. Have them relieved frequently.'

'Right, captain,' replied Mr Mathew.

'I recommend Crockston for this duty. The chap claims to have excellent sight; it's time to put him to the test. Include him in the morning shift and he can keep watch in the early mists. If anything new comes up, have me informed.'

That said, James Playfair retired to his cabin. Mr Mathew had Crockston brought and passed on the captain's orders.

'At six o'clock tomorrow morning,' he said, 'you will go to your observation post in the spars of the foresail.'

By way of response, Crockston gave an affirmative grunt. But hardly had Mr Mathew turned his back than the sailor murmured a number of incomprehensible words and finally exclaimed:

'What the devil does he mean by spars of the foresail?'

At that moment, his nephew John Stiggs joined him on the forecastle.

'Well, how are things, my good Crockston?' he said.

'Fine, fine,' replied the sailor with a forced smile. 'The only thing is that this devil of a boat shakes like a dog getting out of the river and I'm feeling a bit queasy.'

'Poor you!' said the novice, looking at Crockston with a keen sense of gratitude.

'And when I think,' resumed the sailor, 'that I have let myself get seasick at my age! What a weakling I am! But it will all work out! It will all work out! And these spars are also bothering me…'

'Dear Crockston, and it's for me…'

'For you and for him,' replied Crockston. 'But not a word about that, John. Trust in God; he will not abandon you.'

Upon this, John Stiggs and Crockston returned to the sailors' quarters, and the former waited until he had seen the young novice lying peacefully in the narrow cabin that had been reserved for him before he went to sleep.

At six o'clock the next day, Crockston rose to go and take up his post. He went up on deck where the first mate ordered him to climb up into the masts and keep a close watch.

At these words, the sailor seemed a little undecided. Then, making his mind up, he headed towards *The Dolphin*'s stern.

'Where are you going?' cried Mr Mathew.

'Where you're sending me,' replied Crockston.

'I'm telling you to climb up to the spars of the foresail.'

'And that's where I'm going,' replied the sailor unperturbed, continuing to make for the poop deck.

'Are you making fun of me?' Mr Mathew retorted impatiently. 'Going to look for the spars of the foresail on the mizzenmast. You seem to me like a cockney who knows little about braiding cord and splicing! What scow[7] have you sailed on, chum? To the foresail, stupid, to the foresail!'

The watch sailors who had hastened over at the first mate's words were unable to suppress huge roars of laughter when they saw Crockston's disconcerted air as he made his way back towards the forecastle.

'So,' he said, considering the mast whose tip was completely invisible in the morning fog, 'so I have to climb up there?'

'Yes,' replied Mr Mathew, 'and hurry up! By Saint Patrick, a Federal ship will have had time to insert its bowsprit into our rigging before this idler arrives at his post. Will you get going?'

Without saying a word, Crockston hauled himself up onto the rail with difficulty. He then began to climb the ratlines with remarkable clumsiness in the manner of a man who does not know how to use his feet and hands. When he arrived at the top of the foresail, instead of striking out nimbly he remained immobile, clinging onto the tackle with the energy of a person seized by vertigo. Mr Mathew, stunned by such awkwardness and feeling himself overcome by anger, ordered him to come down to the deck that instant.

'That fellow,' he said to the boatswain, 'has never been a sailor in his life. Johnston, go and have a quick look at what he's got in his bag.'

The boatswain made his way quickly to the sailors' quarters.

During this time, Crockston was descending again with difficulty. Losing his footing, he grabbed hold of the loose rigging, which unrolled, and he fell to the deck fairly hard.

'Clumsy oaf, utter boor, freshwater sailor!' cried out Mr Mathew by way of comfort. 'What have you come on board *The Dolphin* for? You made yourself out to be a sturdy sailor, but you can't so much as distinguish between the mizzenmast and the foremast! Well, we're going to have a little talk.'

Crockston did not respond. He braced himself in the manner of a man resigned to the very worst. Just then, the boatswain returned from his visit.

'Here's what I found in this peasant's bag,' he said to the first mate. 'A suspicious file of letters.'

'Give it here,' said Mr Mathew. 'Letters bearing the stamp of the Northern United States! "Mr Halliburtt of Boston!" An abolitionist! A Federal...! Scoundrel! You're nothing but a traitor! You came on board to betray us! Rest assured, your affair is settled; you're going to feel the claws of the cat of nine tails! Boatswain, have the captain informed. You others, keep an eye on this rogue while we're waiting.'

While he was receiving these compliments, Crockston grimaced like an old devil, but he did not open his lips. He had been tied to the capstan and was unable to move either his feet or his hands.

A few minutes later, James Playfair emerged from his cabin and made his way to the forecastle. Mr Mathew immediately filled him in on the matter.

'What have you to say in response?' asked James Playfair, barely containing his irritation.

'Nothing,' replied Crockston.

'And what have you come on board my ship for?'

'Nothing.'

'And what do you expect from me now?'

'Nothing.'

'And who are you? An American, as these letters appear to prove?'

Crockston did not reply.

'Boatswain,' said James Playfair, '50 lashes with the whip to make this man loosen his tongue. Will that be enough, Crockston?'

'We'll see,' replied the novice John Stiggs's uncle without turning a hair.

'Get to it, you others,' said the boatswain.

Upon this order, two strong sailors came to strip Crockston of his woollen pea jacket. They had already seized the formidable instrument and were raising it to the patient's shoulders when the novice John Stiggs rushed onto the deck, pale and dishevelled.

'Captain!' he cried.

'Ah, the nephew!' said James Playfair.

'Captain,' began the novice making a violent effort to control himself, 'I will tell you what Crockston didn't want to tell you! I will not hide what he still wishes to keep silent. Yes, he is American and I am as well. We are both enemies of those in favour of slavery, but we are not traitors who have come on board to betray *The Dolphin* and to deliver her to the Federal ships.'

'What have you come for then?' asked the captain in a severe voice, examining the young novice carefully.

The latter hesitated for a few moments before replying, and then said in a fairly firm voice:

'Captain, I would like to speak to you in private.'

While John Stiggs made this request, James Playfair continued to consider him carefully. The novice's young and gentle face, his singularly pleasant voice, the slenderness and whiteness of his hands, barely concealed under a tanned layer of skin, and his large eyes, which remained gentle despite his animation, all gave rise to a certain idea in the captain's mind. When John Stiggs had made his request, Playfair looked at Crockston fixedly and the latter shrugged his shoulders. He then fixed a questioning look on the novice, which the latter was unable to withstand, and said just one word to him:

'Come.'

John Stiggs followed the captain onto the poop deck where James Playfair, opening the door to his cabin, said to the novice, whose cheeks were pale with emotion:

'Please do come in, miss.'

'Captain,' he said

Thus addressed, John began to redden and two involuntary tears ran from his eyes.

'Don't worry, miss,' said James Playfair in a gentler voice, 'and please inform me of the circumstances to which I owe the honour of having you aboard my ship.'

The young girl hesitated for a moment, then, reassured by the captain's look, she decided to speak.

'Sir,' she said, 'I am going to join my father in Charleston. The city is surrounded by land and blockaded by sea. I didn't know how to enter it, and then I learnt that *The Dolphin* was proposing to run the blockade. So I took passage on board your ship, sir, and I beg you to forgive me for acting without your consent. You would have refused it.'

'Certainly,' replied James Playfair.

'Then I did well not to ask you,' replied the young girl in a firmer voice.

The captain crossed his arms, walked around his cabin and then returned.

'What is your name,' he asked her.

'Jenny Halliburtt.'

'Your father, if I can rely on the address on the letters seized from Crockston, is from Boston?'

'Yes, sir.'

'And a man from the North finds himself in a Southern town at the height of the United States war?'

'My father is a prisoner, sir. He was in Charleston when the first gunshots of the civil war were fired, and when the Union troops found themselves driven out of Fort Sumter by the Confederates. My father's opinions made him an object of hatred for the proslavery side and he was imprisoned on the orders of General Beauregard in defiance of all laws. I was in Britain at the time with a relative who has just died and, finding myself alone with only Crockston, my family's most faithful servant, as support, I wished to join my father and share his prison.'

'And what was Mr Halliburtt?' asked James Playfair.

'A loyal and courageous journalist,' replied Jenny proudly. 'One of the *Tribune*'s[8] most worthy writers and the one to have defended the cause of the blacks most boldly.'

'An abolitionist!' exclaimed the captain violently. 'One of those men who have covered their country with blood and ruins under the vain pretext of abolishing slavery!'

'Sir,' replied Jenny Halliburtt, turning pale, 'you are insulting my father! You should not forget that I am alone here in defending him!'

The young captain's face flushed a vivid red and a mixture of anger and shame took possession of him. It seemed that he was going to reply to the young girl with scant consideration, but he managed to contain himself and opened the door to his cabin.

'Boatswain,' he cried.

The boatswain rushed over immediately.

'From now on, this cabin will belong to Miss Jenny Halliburtt,' he said. 'Have a berth prepared for me at the end of the poop deck. I require nothing more.'

The boatswain looked with astonishment at this young novice with a female name. But, at a sign from James Playfair, he left.

'And now, miss, you find yourself at home,' said *The Dolphin*'s young captain.

Then he withdrew.

4

Crockston's Trick

MISS HALLIBURTT'S STORY was soon known to all of the crew. Crockston made no bones about telling it. Upon the captain's orders, he had been untied from the capstan, and the cat of nine tails had been returned to its home.

'A pleasant creature,' said Crockston, 'especially when it draws its claws in.'

As soon as he was free, he went down to the sailors' quarters, picked up a small case and took it to Miss Jenny. The young girl was able to resume wearing her female apparel, but she remained confined in her cabin and did not reappear on deck.

As for Crockston, it was well and truly established that he was no more a sailor than he was a horse guard, and he had to be exempted from all duties on board.

Nevertheless, *The Dolphin* made rapid progress across the Atlantic, twisting its waves in her twin screws. Operations merely consisted of keeping a careful watch. The day after the scene that betrayed Miss Jenny's secret, James Playfair was pacing rapidly up and down on the poop deck. He had made no attempt to see the young girl again and to resume the conversation he had had with her the day before.

During his walk, he passed Crockston frequently. The

American evidently desired to talk to the captain, examining him shiftily with a satisfied grimace and looking at him with such insistence that the latter finally became irritated.

'What do you want from me now?' James Playfair shouted out to the American. 'You're hanging round me like a swimmer round a buoy! Is there going to be an end to this soon?'

'Forgive me, captain,' Crockston replied squinting, 'but I have something to say to you.'

'Will you say it then?'

'Oh, it's very simple. I just want to say that you're a good man deep down.'

'Why deep down?'

'Deep down and on the surface too.'

'I don't need your compliments.'

'They aren't compliments. I'll wait until you've finished before I pay you any of those.'

'Until I've finished what?'

'Your task.'

'Oh! I have a task to complete?'

'Of course. You've received us on board, the young girl and me. Fine. You've given your cabin to Miss Halliburtt. Good. You've spared me the whip. No one could do more. You're going to take us straight to Charleston. That's wonderful. But it's not all.'

'What! It's not all!' cried James Playfair, stunned at Crockston's claims.

'Certainly not,' replied the latter, assuming a mocking air. 'Her father is a prisoner there!'

'And?'

'And he needs setting free.'

'Free Miss Halliburtt's father?'

'Yes. A worthy man, a courageous citizen! He's worth a risk.'

'Master Crockston,' said James Playfair frowning, 'you strike me as a first-rate joker. But remember this: I am in no mood for jokes.'

'You're mistaken, captain,' replied the American. 'I'm not joking in the slightest. I'm speaking extremely seriously. What I'm proposing may seem absurd at first, but when you have thought about it, you will see that you can do nothing else.'

'What! I have to free Mr Halliburtt?'

'Yes. You will ask General Beauregard to release him and he will not refuse you.'

'And if he does refuse me?'

'Then,' responded Crockston unruffled, 'we'll resort to drastic measures and remove the prisoner from under the Confederates' noses.'

'So,' exclaimed James Playfair, whose anger was beginning to overcome him, 'so, not content with passing through the Federal fleets and running the Charleston blockade, I now have to take to the sea again under cannon fire from the forts, and all to free a gentleman whom I do not know, one of these abolitionists that I hate, one of these inept journalists who spill their ink rather than spilling their blood!'

'Oh, one cannon shot more or less...' added Crockston.

'Master Crockston,' said James Playfair, 'listen carefully. If you make the mistake of speaking to me about this again, I will have you sent to the hold for the entire crossing to teach you to watch your tongue.'

That said, the captain dismissed the American who walked away muttering:

'Well, I'm not dissatisfied with that conversation! We're underway! Everything is going well!'

When James Playfair had said 'an abolitionist that I hate', his tongue had obviously run away from him. He was not a partisan of slavery, but he did not want to admit that the question of servitude was predominant in the United States civil war, despite the formal declarations of President Lincoln. So did he claim that the Southern states – eight out of 36 – theoretically had the right to break away as they had joined together of their own free will? No. He hated the men from the North – that was all there was to it. He hated them as former brothers separated from the common line, as British citizens who had seen fit to do what he, James Playfair, now approved of for the Confederate states. Such were the political views of *The Dolphin*'s captain. But, above all, the war in America was a nuisance to him personally and he bore a grudge against those who were responsible for it. His reaction to this suggestion that he set free an enemy of slavery, thereby turning the Confederates, with whom he hoped to trade, against himself, can thus be understood.

Nevertheless, Crockston's insinuations kept bothering him. He cast them far away, but they never failed to return and assail his mind. The next day, when Miss Jenny came up on deck for a moment, he did not dare to look her in the face.

This was certainly a great pity, as this young girl with blonde hair and gentle, intelligent eyes deserved to be looked at by a young man of 30. But James felt embarrassed in her presence; he sensed that this charming creature had a strong and generous soul that had been shaped by misfortune. He understood that his silence where she was concerned was based on a refusal to acquiesce with her dearest wishes. Moreover, Jenny did not seek out James Playfair, though neither did she avoid him, and during the first few days they spoke little or not at all. Miss Halliburtt scarcely left her cabin, and she would certainly never have said a word to *The Dolphin*'s captain had it not been for Crockston's stratagem, which pitted them against one another.

The worthy American was a faithful servant of the Halliburtt family. He had been raised in his master's house and his devotion knew no bounds. His common sense equalled his courage and his vigour. As we have seen, he had his own way of viewing things. He created a particular philosophy on events and did not allow himself to get discouraged. In the most unfortunate of circumstances, he had a marvellous capacity for pulling through.

This good man had got it into his head to free Mr Halliburtt, to use the captain's ship and the captain himself to save him, and to return to Scotland. Such was his plan, though the young girl had no other aim than to join her father and to share his captivity. And so Crockston attempted to woo James Playfair; he had fired his broadside, as we have seen, but the enemy had not surrendered. On the contrary.

'Come,' he said to himself, 'it is absolutely essential that Miss Jenny and the captain end up getting along. If they sulk like this for the entire crossing, we'll get nowhere. They have to talk, discuss, argue even, just as long as they speak. I'll be damned if, during the course of the conversation, James Playfair doesn't finish up suggesting what he's currently refusing to do.'

But when Crockston saw that the young girl and the young man were avoiding each other, he began to feel uneasy.

'I must hurry things along,' he said to himself.

Thus, on the morning of the fourth day, he entered Miss Halliburtt's cabin rubbing his hands with an air of perfect satisfaction.

'Good news' he cried, 'good news! You'll never guess what the captain suggested to me. A very worthy young man!'

'Oh!' replied Jenny, her heart beating violently, 'What has he suggested?'

'Freeing Mr Halliburtt, releasing him from the Confederates and taking him back to Scotland.'

'Truly?' cried Jenny.

'It's as I'm telling you, miss. What a kind-hearted man James Playfair is! But that's what the British are like: all bad or all good! Yes, that man can count on my gratitude; I would die for him if it would be of service.'

Jenny's joy upon hearing Crockston's words was great. Free her father! She would never have dared to conceive of such a project! And *The Dolphin*'s captain was going to risk his ship and his crew for her!

'That's what he's like,' added Crockston, 'and that, Miss Jenny, is worthy of your thanks.'

'Better than thanks,' cried the young girl, 'eternal friendship!'

And she left her cabin immediately to find James Playfair and express the sentiments with which her heart was overflowing.

'We're making progress,' murmured the American. 'In fact we're racing along. We'll get there!'

James Playfair was walking on the poop deck and, as might be imagined, was extremely surprised, not to say astonished, to see the young girl approach and hold out her hand to him, her eyes moist with tears of gratitude.

'Thank you, sir, thank you for your devotion. I would never have dared expect it from a stranger!'

'Miss,' replied the captain in the manner of a man who did not and could not understand, 'I don't know...'

'And yet, sir,' resumed Jenny, 'you are going to brave a great many dangers for me, perhaps compromise your own interests. You have already done so much by offering me hospitality on your ship to which I had no right...'

'Forgive me, Miss Jenny,' replied James Playfair, 'but I swear to you that I do not understand your words. I have behaved towards you as any well-brought-up young man would towards a woman, and my manner of acting does not merit such recognition or such thanks.'

'Mr Playfair,' said Jenny, 'it is useless to pretend any longer. Crockston has told me everything!'

'Oh!' said the captain, 'Crockston has told you everything. Then I understand less and less what motive made you leave your cabin and come here to have me listen to words that...'

Thus speaking, the captain felt rather ill-at-ease. He was remembering the blunt manner in which he had welcomed the American's overtures. Luckily for him, however, Jenny did not leave him time for further explanations and interrupted him, saying:

Mr James, when I took passage on board your ship, I had no other design than to go to Charleston where, however cruel those in favour of slavery are, they would not have refused to let a poor girl share her father's prison. That was all, and I would never have hoped for an impossible

'Thank you, sir, thank you'

return, but as your generosity extends to wishing to free
my imprisoned father, as you want to attempt everything
to save him, rest assured of my fervent gratitude and
allow me to give you my hand!

James did not know what to say or what attitude to take.
He bit his lips. He did not dare to take the hand that the
young girl held out to him. He saw that Crockston had
compromised him and that it was impossible for him to step
back. And yet helping to free Mr Halliburtt and getting
mixed up in a nasty piece of business did not form part of
his plans. But how could he betray the hopes of this young
girl? How could he refuse this hand that she held out to him
with such a strong feeling of friendship? How could he
change the tears of gratitude that escaped from her eyes into
tears of grief?

The young man thus tried to answer evasively in a
manner that preserved his freedom of action and did not
commit him to anything in the future.

'Miss Jenny,' he said, 'believe me when I say that I will
do anything in the world to...'

And he took Jenny's small hand in his hands, but at the
gentle pressure, he felt his heart melt and his head become
fuzzy, and the words to express his thoughts failed him. He
stammered out a few vague words:

'Miss...Miss Jenny...for you...'

Crockston, who was watching, grinned and rubbed his
hands together, repeating:

'Getting there! Getting there! There we are!'

How could James Playfair get himself out of this embar-
rassing situation? Nobody could have said. But luckily for him,
if not for *The Dolphin*, the voice of the look-out was heard.

'Hullo there, officer of the watch!' he cried.

'What is it?' replied Mr Mathew.

'A sail windward!'

Leaving the young girl immediately, James Playfair made his way quickly to the shrouds of the mizzenmast.

5

Cannonballs from *The Iroquois* and Miss Jenny's Arguments

UP TO THAT POINT, *The Dolphin* had advanced remarkably quickly and had enjoyed considerable good fortune. Not a single ship had been sighted before this sail was reported by the look-out.

The Dolphin was then at a latitude of 32° 15' and at a longitude of 57° 43' to the west of the Greenwich Meridian, that is to say three-fifths of the way through her journey. For 48 hours, the ocean's waters had been covered by fog, which was now beginning to lift. While this fog aided *The Dolphin* by concealing her course, it also prevented her from observing a vast area of the sea. Without suspecting it, she could be sailing alongside the ships that she was looking to avoid.

Now this is exactly what had happened, and when the ship was reported she was no more than three nautical miles[9] windward.

When James Playfair reached the spars, he made out a large Federal corvette in the thinning fog, sailing full steam ahead. It was heading towards *The Dolphin* so as to cut across her path.

After examining her carefully, the captain came back down onto the deck and had his first mate join him.

'Mr Mathew,' he said to him, 'what do you think of this ship?'

'I think, captain, that she's a Federal navy vessel that suspects our intentions.'

'Yes, there's no possible doubt as to her nationality,' replied James Playfair. 'See.'

At that moment, the star-studded flag of the Northern United States was hoisted to the corvette's gaff, backed up by a cannon shot.

'An invitation to show our colours,' said Mr Mathew. 'Well, let's show them. We've nothing to be ashamed of.'

'What's the use?' replied James Playfair. 'Our flag will not offer us any real protection and it will not prevent these people from wanting to pay us a visit. No. Let's forge ahead.'

'And let's go quickly,' resumed Mr Mathew, 'If my eyes don't deceive me, I've seen this corvette before near Liverpool where she'd come to monitor the vessels under construction. May I lose my good name if the board on her taffrail[10] doesn't read *The Iroquois*.'

'And she's a swift vessel?'

'One of the best in the Federal navy.'

'What cannons does she have?'

'Eight cannons.'

'Pooh!'

'Oh, don't shrug your shoulders, captain,' replied Mr Mathew in a serious tone. 'Of those eight cannons, two of them pivot. There's a sixty-pound one on the quarter-deck and a hundred-pound one on the deck, both of which are rifled.'

'Gracious!' said James Playfair, 'Those are Parrotts. They have a range of three nautical miles, those cannons.'

'Yes, captain, and even better.'

He made out a large Federal corvette

'Well, Mr Mathew, whether the cannons are one-hundred pound or four pound, whether they have a range of three nautical miles or of 500 yards, it's all one if you move fast enough to avoid their cannonballs. We'll show *The Iroquois* how a ship sails when it's made for sailing. Have the fires stoked up, Mr Mathew.'

The first mate passed on the captain's orders to the engineer, and black smoke soon swirled above the steamer's funnels.

These symptoms did not appear to be to the corvette's liking, as she signalled to *The Dolphin* to heave to. But James Playfair did not take any notice of the warning and did not change the direction of his ship.

'And now,' he said, 'we'll see what *The Iroquois* will do. It's a good opportunity for her to try out her hundred-pound cannon and to discover its range. Full steam ahead!'

'All right!' said Mr Mathew. 'It won't be long before we're treated to a nice greeting.'

Returning to the poop deck, the captain saw Miss Halliburtt sitting calmly near the handrail.

'Miss Jenny,' he said to her, 'we are probably going to be chased by this corvette that you can see windward and, as she will use cannon fire to communicate with us, I would like to offer you my arm to escort you back to your cabin.'

'Thank you, Mr Playfair,' replied the young girl, looking at the young man, 'but I am not scared of cannon fire.'

'Nevertheless, miss, despite the distance, there may be some danger.'

'Oh, I haven't been brought up to be timid. They accustom us to everything in America, and I assure you that the cannonballs of *The Iroquois* will not make me lower my head.'

'You are brave, Miss Jenny.'

'Let's accept that I am brave, Mr Playfair, and allow me to remain with you.'

'I cannot refuse you anything, Miss Halliburtt,' replied the captain, considering the young girl's calm assurance.

He had barely finished speaking when they saw white smoke shoot out of the Federal corvette's bulwark. Before the noise of the detonation had reached *The Dolphin*, a cylindro-conical projectile, spinning round and round in the air with horrifying rapidity in a screw-like motion, headed towards the steamer. It was easy to follow its progress, which was relatively slow, as projectiles leave the mouths of rifled cannons less quickly than from any other smoothbore cannon.

Twenty fathoms from *The Dolphin*, the projectile, its trajectory falling appreciably, skimmed the waves, marking its passage with a succession of jets of water. When it touched the liquid surface, it gained new momentum and rebounded to quite a height, passing above *The Dolphin*, cutting the starboard arm of the foreyard, falling back down thirty fathoms beyond and sinking into the waves.

'Dash it!' said James Playfair. 'Get to it, get to it! It won't be long until the second shot.'

'Oh!' said Mr Mathew, 'It will take a while to recharge cannons like that.'

'Well, this is a very interesting sight,' said Crockston, who was watching the scene unfold with his arms crossed in the manner of a perfectly disinterested spectator. 'And to think that it's our friends who are firing on us like that!'

'Oh, it's you!' exclaimed James Playfair, looking the American up and down from head to toe.

'It's me, captain,' replied the American unperturbed.

'I've come to see how these brave Federals fire. Not bad, actually, not bad!'

The captain was about to reply to Crockston in no uncertain terms, but at that moment a second projectile struck the sea across the starboard quarter.

'Good!' shouted James Playfair. 'We've already gained two cable's lengths on *The Iroquois*. They move like a buoy, your friends, do you hear, Master Crockston?'

'I don't deny it,' replied the American, 'and for the first time in my life, it doesn't fail to cause me pleasure.'

A third shot remained far behind the first two, and in less than ten minutes *The Dolphin* was out of the range of the corvette's cannons.

'That's worth all the patent logs in the world, Mr Mathew,' said James Playfair. 'Thanks to these shots, we have a good idea of our speed. Now, have the fires damped down. There's no point in burning our fuel unnecessarily.'

'You are in command of a good ship,' said Miss Halliburtt to the young captain.

'Yes, Miss Jenny, she sails at seventeen knots, my fine *Dolphin*. We'll have lost sight of this Federal corvette before the end of the day.'

James Playfair was not exaggerating the nautical qualities of his vessel and the sun had not yet set when the top of the American ship's masts disappeared below the horizon.

This incident enabled the captain to perceive Miss Halliburtt's character in a new light. Moreover, the ice had been broken. For the rest of the crossing, the meetings between *The Dolphin*'s captain and his passenger were frequent and prolonged. He found her to be a calm, strong, thoughtful and intelligent young girl who spoke with great frankness in an American manner. She had firm ideas on all things and expressed them with a conviction that touched James Playfair's heart, though without his knowing. She loved her country; she was passionate about the great idea of the Union and expressed her opinion on the war in the United States with an enthusiasm that no other woman would have been capable of. Thus it was that James Playfair was more than once at a loss as to how to respond to her. Often, the opinions of the 'merchant' came into play, and Jenny attacked them with no less vigour and did not wish to compromise at all. At first, James argued a lot. He tried to support the Confederates against the Federals, to prove that the secessionists were in the right and to affirm that people who had come together voluntarily could separate in the same manner. But the young girl was not willing to yield on this point. Moreover, she demonstrated that the question of slavery took precedence over all others in this battle of the North against the South, and that it was much more about morality and humanity than politics. James was beaten without being able to reply. Furthermore, he mainly listened during these discussions. Whether he was more affected by Miss Halliburtt's arguments or by the charm of listening to her is almost impossible to say. But finally, he was forced to acknowledge that the question of slavery was a primary issue in the United States war and that it was essential to bring it to a definitive close and to put an end to these final horrors of barbarian times.

Besides, as has been said, the captain's political opinions did not worry him a great deal. He would have sacrificed more serious ones to arguments presented in such a captivating manner and in similar conditions. He thus set little store by his ideas on this subject. But that was not all. The dearest interests of the 'merchant' were finally attacked directly. In other words, the question of the trade for which *The Dolphin* was destined and the subject of the munitions that she was carrying to the Confederates.

'Yes, Mr James,' Miss Halliburtt said to him one day, 'gratitude will not prevent me from speaking to you with complete frankness. Quite the contrary. You are a fine sailor and a skilled trader, and the honourable nature of the Playfair firm is held up as an example, but, at this moment, it is failing to adhere to its principles and is not engaging in a trade worthy of it.'

'What!' exclaimed James, 'The Playfair firm doesn't have the right to attempt a commercial operation of this kind!'

'No! It is taking war munitions to unfortunate individuals in revolt against the legitimate government of their country, and it is giving arms to a bad cause.'

'Well, Miss Jenny,' replied the captain, 'I will not discuss the right of the Confederates with you. I will reply with one word only: I am a merchant and, as such, I am only concerned with the interests of my company. I look for profit wherever it's to be found.'

'Which is exactly what is blameful, Mr James,' resumed the young girl. 'Profit is no excuse. You are just as guilty at this moment by providing the people from the South with the means to continue a criminal war as you would be were you to sell the Chinese the opium that stupefies them!'

'Oh! This time, Miss Jenny, that's too strong, and I cannot admit...'

'No, what I am saying is fair, and when you take a look at yourself, when you understand the role that you are playing, when you think of the results that you are responsible for in the eyes of all, you will acknowledge that I am right on this point as on so many others.'

At these words, James Playfair remained stunned. He left the young girl, seething with anger and sensing his inability to respond. He sulked like a child for half an hour, an hour at most, and then returned to this singular young girl who overwhelmed him with her surest arguments and such an amiable smile.

In short, despite everything and although he did not wish to acknowledge it, Captain James Playfair's life was no longer his own. He was no longer second only to God on board his ship.

Thus, to Crockston's great joy, it seemed that Mr Halliburtt's affairs were making good progress. The captain appeared to have made up his mind to do anything to free Miss Jenny's father, even if it meant compromising *The Dolphin*, her cargo and her crew, and incurring the wrath of his worthy Uncle Vincent.

6

The Sullivan's Island Channel

TWO DAYS AFTER the meeting with *The Iroquois*, *The Dolphin* found herself abreast of the Bermudas, where she met with a violent squall. These waters are frequently visited by hurricanes of extreme vehemence. They are famed for their disasters, and it is here that Shakespeare set the stirring scenes of his drama *The Tempest*, in which Ariel and Caliban fight for control of the waves.

It was a terrible gale. James Playfair thought for a minute about putting into port at Mainland, one of the Bermudas, where the British have a military post. It would have been an annoying and unfortunate delay. Luckily, *The Dolphin* performed wonderfully during the storm, and, after spending an entire day fleeing the hurricane, she was able to resume her route towards the American coast.

But if James Playfair had shown himself satisfied with his ship, he had been no less delighted by the courage and composure of the young girl. Miss Halliburtt spent the worst hours of the hurricane beside him on the deck. After considerable reflection, James saw that a profound, imperious and irresistible love was taking possession of his entire being.

'Yes,' he said to himself, 'this brave girl is mistress on my ship! She shakes me as the sea shakes a vessel in distress.

The gale

I can feel myself sinking! What will Uncle Vincent say? Oh, feeble nature! I am certain that if Jenny asked me to throw the whole of this accursed contraband cargo into the sea, I would do it without hesitating out of love for her!'

Luckily for Playfair and Co., Miss Halliburtt did not demand this sacrifice. Nevertheless, the poor captain was overcome, and Crockston, who read his heart like an open book, rubbed his hands until they were almost raw.

'We have him, we have him!' he repeated to himself. 'My master will be safely installed on board in *The Dolphin*'s best cabin before eight days have passed!'

So was Miss Jenny aware of the sentiments that she inspired? Did she go so far as to return them? Nobody could have said. James Playfair least of all. Although under the influence of her American education, the young girl maintained a perfect reserve and her secret remained deeply buried within her heart.

While love was making such progress in the soul of her young captain, *The Dolphin* was sailing with no less rapidity towards Charleston.

On 13 January, the lookout signalled land ten nautical miles to the west. The coastline was low and hard to distinguish from the line of the waves at that distance. Crockston examined the horizon carefully and, at about nine o'clock in the morning, focussing on a point in the brightening sky, exclaimed:

'Charleston's lighthouse!'

Had *The Dolphin* arrived at night, this lighthouse, situated on Morris Island and rising up 140 feet above sea level, would have been noticed several hours earlier, as the beams from its revolving light are visible 14 nautical miles away.[11]

Having thereby established *The Dolphin*'s position, James Playfair had only one thing to do: decide which channel to take to enter Charleston Bay.

'If we meet with no obstacles,' he said, 'we will be safe in the port's docks within three hours.'

The city of Charleston is situated at the end of an estuary measuring seven nautical miles in length and two nautical miles in width. The estuary is called Charleston Harbour and is fairly difficult to enter. The entrance is squeezed between Morris Island to the south and Sullivan's Island[12] to the north. At the time when *The Dolphin* was attempting to run the blockade, Morris Island already belonged to the Federal troops, and General Gillmore had had batteries established there to scour and control the harbour. In contrast, Sullivan's Island was in the hands of the Confederates, who were standing firm in Fort Moultrie, situated at its tip. There was thus every advantage for *The Dolphin* in staying close to the northern banks to avoid the fire from the batteries on Morris Island.

Five channels allowed access to the estuary: the Sullivan's Island channel, the north channel, the Overall channel, the main channel and, finally, the Lawford channel. But the latter was not to be attempted by strangers, unless they had excellent practical experience on board, or by ships drawing less than seven feet of water. As for the north channel and the Overall channel, they were strung with Federal batteries and could not be considered. Had James Playfair been able to choose, he would have taken his steamer down the main channel, which is the best and whose bearings are easy to follow, but it was necessary to yield to circumstances and to decide according to events. Moreover, *The Dolphin*'s captain

Crockston scanned the horizon attentively

was perfectly aware of all the secrets of this bay, its dangers, the depth of its waters at low tide, its currents. He was thus capable of steering his vessel with perfect assurance once they had entered one of these narrow straits. The crux of the matter was getting into one.

Now this manoeuvre required vast experience of the sea and precise knowledge of *The Dolphin*'s qualities.

In fact, two Federal frigates were then cruising in the waters of Charleston. Mr Mathew soon brought them to James Playfair's attention.

'They are getting ready,' he said, 'to ask us what we are doing in these parts.'

'Well, we won't respond,' replied the captain, 'and their curiosity will go unrewarded.'

Nevertheless, the cruisers headed towards *The Dolphin* full steam ahead. The latter continued its journey, taking care to keep out of the range of their cannons. However, so as to gain time, James Playfair headed south-west, hoping to put the enemy boats off the scent. The idea was to have them believe that *The Dolphin* was intending to head into the Morris Island channels. There were batteries and cannons there that would require just one shot to sink the British boat. The Federals thus allowed *The Dolphin* to sail south-west, being content to observe her and not pursuing her too vigorously.

For one hour, the respective situation of the ships did not change. Moreover, James Playfair, wishing to deceive the cruisers about *The Dolphin*'s speed, had had the slide valve altered and was not sailing at full steam. However, given the thick whirls of smoke that were escaping from her funnels, people would think that she was looking to obtain maximum pressure and, consequently, maximum speed.

'They will be extremely surprised soon,' said James Playfair, 'when they see us slip through their hands!'

In fact, when the captain found himself fairly close to Morris Island and facing a line of cannons whose range he was unsure of, he suddenly changed course, making his ship turn back on herself and heading back towards the north, leaving the cruisers two nautical miles windward. The latter, seeing this manoeuvre and understanding the steamer's plans, set about pursuing her resolutely. But it was too late. The Dolphin, doubling her speed and with her screws working at full force, quickly left them behind and drew closer to the coast. A few cannon shots were levelled at her just to make certain, but the Federal projectiles were in vain and only reached halfway. At 11 o'clock in the morning, the steamer, sailing close to Sullivan's Island thanks to her shallow draft, headed full steam ahead into the narrow channel where she was safe. No Federal cruiser would have dared to follow her into this channel, which has an average of less than 11 feet of water at low tide.

'What!' cried Crockston, 'It's as easy as all that?'

'Oh!' exclaimed James Playfair, 'The difficulty, Master Crockston, is not entering, but leaving.'

'Pooh!' replied the American. 'I'm not really worried about that. With a ship like The Dolphin and a captain like Mr James Playfair, you can enter when you like and leave too.'

Nevertheless, James Playfair, telescope in hand, carefully examined the route that they were to follow. He had excellent coastal maps to consult that enabled him to sail onwards without any trouble or hesitation.

Once his ship had entered the narrow channel that runs alongside Sullivan's Island, James steered by positioning the middle of Fort Moultrie to the west by half north until Castle Pickney, recognisable by its dark colour and situated on the isolated island of Shute's Folly, appeared to the north-north-east. On the other side, he kept the Fort Johnson building, high on the left, at an angle of two degrees to the north of Fort Sumter.

At that moment, they were greeted by several cannon shots from the batteries on Morris Island, which failed to reach them. They thus continued on their way without deviating by one point, passed in front of Moultrieville, situated at the tip of Sullivan's Island, and emerged into the bay.

They soon left Fort Sumter on their left and were masked by it from the Federal batteries.

This fort, famous in the United States war, is situated three-and-a-third nautical miles from Charleston[13] and around one nautical mile from each side of the bay. It is a truncated pentagon constructed on an artificial island in granite from Massachusetts. It took ten years to build and cost more than nine hundred thousand dollars.

It is this fort that Anderson and the Federal troops were chased out of on 13 April 1861, and it is against it that the first of the separatists' shots was fired. It is impossible to estimate the amount of iron and lead that the cannons of the Federals showered down on it. Nevertheless, it resisted for almost three years. Several months after *The Dolphin*'s crossing, it fell under the fire of 300 pounds of rifled Parrott cannons that General Gillmore had established on Morris Island.

But it was now at full strength and the Confederates' flag flew above this enormous stone pentagon.

Once they had passed the fort, the town of Charleston

appeared, lying between the Ashley River and the Cooper River and forming an advanced point on the harbour.

James Playfair sailed between the buoys that mark the channel, leaving Charleston lighthouse to the south-south-west, visible above the embankments of Morris Island. He had hoisted the British flag to *The Dolphin*'s gaff, and she made her way through the channels at a marvellous speed.

When she had left the quarantine buoy on the starboard side, she advanced freely to the centre of the bay. Miss Halliburtt was standing on the poop deck, studying this town where her father was kept a prisoner, and her eyes filled with tears.

Finally, the steamer's speed was moderated upon her captain's orders. *The Dolphin* sailed past the southern and eastern batteries on the point and was soon moored at the quay in the North Commercial Wharf.

7

A Southern General

WHEN SHE ARRIVED at the quay in Charleston, *The Dolphin* was greeted by a vast and cheering crowd. The inhabitants of this city, strictly blockaded by sea, were not accustomed to visits from European ships. They wondered in amazement what this large steamer, proudly flying the British flag at her gaff, was doing in their waters. But when they discovered the aim of her voyage and why she had run the Sullivan's Island channel, and when the rumour spread that the cargo contained within her flanks consisted of contraband war goods, the applause and cries of joy doubled in intensity.

James Playfair got in touch with General Beauregard, the city's military commander, without a moment's delay. The latter was all too willing to receive *The Dolphin*'s young captain, who had arrived at exactly the right time to provide his soldiers with the clothing and munitions that they needed so desperately. It was thus agreed that the ship would be unloaded immediately, and countless pairs of arms appeared to help the British sailors.

Before leaving his vessel, James Playfair had received the most pressing of recommendations from Miss Halliburtt on the subject of her father. The young captain had placed himself entirely at the young girl's service.

'Miss Jenny,' he had said, 'you can count on me. I will

do the impossible to save your father, but I am hoping that this matter will not present any difficulties. I will go to see General Beauregard this very day. Though I will not abruptly request Mr Halliburtt's freedom, I will find out his situation and whether he is free on parole or a prisoner.'

'My poor father!' replied Miss Jenny with a sigh. 'He is unaware that his daughter is so near him. If only I could fly into his arms!'

'Have a little patience, Miss Jenny. You will soon embrace your father. You can rely on me to act with the utmost devotion, but prudently and carefully.'

Thus it was that after dealing with his company's business, delivering *The Dolphin*'s cargo to the general and purchasing an immense stock of cotton at a low price, James Playfair, faithful to his promise, brought the conversation around to the events of the day.

'So,' he said to General Beauregard, 'you believe that the pro-slavery states will triumph?'

'I don't doubt our final victory for a moment. As for Charleston, Lee's army will soon put a stop to the besieging of it. Besides, what do you expect from the abolitionists? Even supposing – and this will not happen – that the commercial cities of Virginia, the two Carolinas, Georgia, Alabama and Mississippi were to fall under their power, what then? Would they be masters of a country that they will never be able to occupy? Certainly not. In my view, were they ever to emerge victorious, their victory would put them in a difficult position.'

'And you are absolutely sure of your soldiers?' asked the captain. 'You don't fear that Charleston will tire of a siege that is ruining it?'

'No! I don't fear betrayal. Besides, the traitors would be sacrificed without pity. I would destroy the city itself by fire or by sword were I to discover the smallest unionist movement. Jefferson Davis entrusted Charleston to me, and you can consider Charleston in safe hands.'

'Do you have any prisoners from the North?' asked James Playfair, arriving at the important object of the conversation.

'Yes, captain,' replied the general. 'The first shot of the scission was fired at Charleston, and the abolitionists who were here tried to resist. After they were beaten, they became prisoners of war.'

'And are there many of them?'

'Around a hundred.'

'Free to roam the city?'

'They were until I discovered a plot they had formed. Their leader had managed to establish contact with the besiegers who were informed about the situation in the city. So I was forced to have these dangerous guests locked up. Several of these Federals will leave their prison only to climb up onto the citadel's ramp where ten Confederate bullets will get the better of their Federalism.'

'What! Shot!' exclaimed the young captain, shuddering in spite of himself.

'Yes! And their leader first of all. A very determined and very dangerous man in a besieged city. I have sent his correspondence to the President's office in Richmond, and his fate will be irrevocably sealed within a week.'

'Who is this man that you're speaking about?' asked James Playfair with a perfect lack of concern.

'A journalist from Boston, a fanatical abolitionist, the damned soul of Lincoln.'

'And his name?'

'Jonathon Halliburtt.'

'Poor devil!' said James Playfair, containing his emotion. 'Whatever he has done, you can't help but pity him. And you think he will be shot?'

'I'm sure of it,' replied Beauregard. 'What do you expect? War is war. You defend yourself as you can.'

'Well, it doesn't concern me,' replied the captain. 'I'll be far away by the time this execution takes place.'

'What! You're thinking of leaving again already?'

'Yes, general. I'm a merchant above all else. As soon as my cotton has been loaded, I'll be taking to the sea. I've entered Charleston, fine, but we have to leave again. That's the important part. *The Dolphin* is a good ship, she could beat all of the Federal navy vessels in a race, but however fast she is, she cannot claim to outstrip one cannonball in a hundred, and a cannonball in her hull or her engine would wreck my commercial scheme.'

'Suit yourself, captain,' replied Beauregard. 'I have no advice for you in such a situation. You're doing your job and you're right to do so. In your place, I would act as you are acting. Besides, life in Charleston isn't very pleasant, and a harbour where it rains bombs three days out of four is not a safe haven for a ship. Leave when it pleases you, but answer this simple question: how many Federal ships are cruising in front of Charleston and how strong are they?'

James Playfair satisfied the general's questions as well as possible and took his leave of him on the best of terms. He then returned to *The Dolphin*, very anxious and very distressed by what he had just learnt.

'What shall I say to Miss Jenny?' he thought. 'Do I have

to tell her about Mr Halliburtt's terrible situation? Would it be better to leave her ignorant of the dangers threatening him? Poor girl!'

He had not taken 50 steps outside the governor's house when he collided with Crockston. The worthy American had been watching for him since his departure.

'Well, captain?'

James Playfair looked at Crockston fixedly, and the latter understood quite clearly that the captain did not have favourable news to give him.

'Did you see Beauregard?' he asked.

'Yes,' replied James Playfair.

'And did you speak to him about Mr Halliburtt?'

'No, he spoke about him to me.'

'Well, captain?'

'Well...I know I can tell you everything, Crockston.'

'Everything, captain.'

'Well, General Beauregard told me that your master will be shot within a week.'

Another man would have fumed with rage at this news or would have given way to a blaze of compromising grief, but the American, who had some nerve, had what looked like a smile on his lips and simply said:

'Pooh! What does it matter?'

'What! What does it matter?' cried James Playfair. 'I tell you that Mr Halliburtt will be shot within a week and you reply "What does it matter!"'

'Yes, if he is on board *The Dolphin* in six days and if *The Dolphin* is in the middle of the ocean in seven.'

'Yes!' said *The Dolphin*'s captain, shaking Crockston's hand. 'I understand you, my good fellow. You're a man of resolution, and I, despite Uncle Vincent and *The Dolphin*'s cargo, would have myself blown up for Miss Jenny.'

'No-one has to be blown up,' replied the American. 'Only the fish would benefit from that. The important thing is to free Mr Halliburtt.'

'But you do know that that will be difficult?'

'Bah!' exclaimed Crockston.

'We will have to communicate with a heavily guarded prisoner.'

'Undoubtedly.'

'And carry out an almost miraculous escape!'

'Pooh!' said Crockston. 'A prisoner is more possessed with the idea of escaping than his guard is with the idea of guarding him. So a prisoner must always succeed in running away. All the odds are in his favour. Which is why, thanks to our actions, Mr Halliburtt will escape.'

'You're right, Crockston.'

'Every time'

'But how will you manage? We need a plan; there are precautions to take.'

'I will think about it.'

'But Miss Jenny, when she learns that her father is condemned to death and that the order for his execution may arrive from one day to the next...'

'She will not learn of it, that's all there is to it.'

'Yes, she must not know. That is best – for her and for us.'

'Where is Mr Halliburtt shut up?' asked Crockston.

'In the citadel,' replied James Playfair.

'Perfect. Now let's go on board!'

'On board, Crockston!'

8

The Escape

MISS JENNY, SEATED ON *The Dolphin*'s poop deck, awaited the captain's return with a mixture of anxiety and impatience. When he joined her, she was unable to utter a single word, but her eyes interrogated James Playfair more ardently than her lips would have done.

The latter, aided by Crockston, only revealed the facts relating to her father's imprisonment to the young girl. He told her that he had carefully sounded out Beauregard about his prisoners of war. As the general did not seem well disposed to them in his view, he had maintained his reserve and would act according to the circumstances.

'Since Mr Halliburtt is not free to move around within the city, his escape will present more of a difficulty. But I will achieve my goal, and I swear to you, Miss Jenny, that *The Dolphin* will not leave Charleston's harbour without your father on board.'

'Thank you, Mr James,' said Jenny. 'Thank you with all my soul.'

Upon these words, James Playfair felt his heart leap within his chest. He moved closer to the young girl, his eyes moist and his voice trembling. Perhaps he was about to speak, to confess the feelings that he was no longer able to contain, when Crockston intervened.

Jenny stood on the poop deck

'That's not all,' he said, 'and this is not the time to get emotional. Let's talk.'

'Do you have a plan, Crockston?' the young girl asked.

'I always have a plan,' replied the American. 'It's my speciality.'

'But a good one?' said James Playfair.

'An excellent one; all the ministers in Washington couldn't come up with anything better. It's as if Mr Halliburtt were on board.'

Crockston said these things with so much assurance and, at the same time, such perfect affability that only the most incredulous of men would have failed to share his conviction.

'We're listening, Crockston,' said James Playfair.

'Good. You, captain, you are going to go to General Beauregard and ask him for a favour that he will not refuse you.'

'What?'

'You will tell him that you have a bad character on board, an out-and-out rogue who is bothering you and who caused the crew to revolt during the crossing, in short an abominable customer. You will ask permission to lock him away in the citadel, though upon the condition that you can take him away again when you depart so as to return to Britain and hand him over to the law in your country.'

'Fine!' replied James Playfair, half smiling. 'I will do all of that, and Beauregard will be happy to comply with my request.'

'I'm perfectly sure of it,' replied the American.

'But,' resumed Playfair, 'there is one thing missing.'

'What?'

'The rogue.'

'I swear to you, Miss Jenny'

'He's standing in front of you, captain.'

'What, that abominable character...?'

'Is me, whether you like it or not.'

'Oh! Brave and noble man!' cried Jenny, squeezing the American's rough hands with her small ones.

'Fine, Crockston,' resumed James Playfair, 'I understand you, my friend, and I only regret one thing – that I am not able to take your place!'

'Each to his own role,' replied Crockston. 'Were you to put yourself in my place, you would be very ill-at-ease, and I will not be. You will have enough to do later getting out of the harbour under fire from the Federals and Confederates. I would make a very bad job of that.'

'Very well, Crockston. Continue.'

'Right. Once in the citadel – I know it – I will see what I need to do, but you can be certain that I will do it well. During this time, you will proceed to load your ship.'

'Oh, business!' said the captain. 'It's a detail of little importance now.'

'Not at all! And Uncle Vincent? What would he say? Let's have sentiment and commercial operations working hand-in-hand. It will prevent suspicion. But let's work quickly. Can you be ready in six days?'

'Yes.'

'Well, have *The Dolphin* loaded and ready to leave on the day of the 22nd.'

'She'll be ready.'

'Listen carefully, on the evening of 22 January send a boat with your best men to White Point at the edge of the city. Wait until nine o'clock and you will see Mr Halliburtt and yours truly appear.'

'But how will you help set Mr Halliburtt free and escape yourself?'

'That's my concern.'

'Dear Crockston,' said Miss Jenny, 'so you are going to risk your life to save my father!'

'Don't worry about me, Miss Jenny, I'm risking absolutely nothing, you can believe me.'

'Well,' asked James Playfair, 'when must we have you locked away?'

'This very day. You see, I'm demoralising your crew. There's no time to lose.'

'Do you want some gold? It may be of use to you in the citadel.'

'Gold to buy a gaoler? No! It's too dear and too simple. When it comes to it, the gaoler keeps the money and the prisoner. And he's right to do so! No! I have other, more certain methods. But some dollars. I have to be able to drink if necessary.'

'And get the gaoler tipsy.'

'No, a tipsy gaoler compromises everything! No, I tell you I have an idea. Let me get on with it.'

'Here, my good Crockston. Here's ten dollars.'

'It's too much, but I'll give you back what's left.'

'Well, are you ready?'

'All set to be an arrant rascal.'

'Let's go then.'

'Crockston,' said the young girl in a voice trembling with emotion, 'Crockston, you are the best man on earth!'

'That wouldn't surprise me,' replied the American with a guffaw. 'Ah, by the way, captain, an important recommendation.'

'What's that?'

'If the general were to propose that you have your scoundrel hung – you know soldiers, they don't beat about the bush!'

'Well, Crockston?'

'Well, you would ask to think about it.'

'I promise.'

That same day, to the tremendous astonishment of the crew who were not privy to the secret, Crockston, irons on his feet and hands, was taken ashore in the middle of ten or so sailors and, half an hour later at the request of Captain James Playfair, the rogue made his way through the city's streets and, despite his resistance, found himself imprisoned in Charleston's citadel.

Over that day and the following days, *The Dolphin* was unloaded in a bustle of activity. The steam cranes worked unceasingly to remove all of the European cargo to make way for the local cargo. The population of Charleston witnessed this interesting operation, helping and congratulating the sailors. It could be said that these good fellows had pride of place; the Southerners held them in high esteem, but James Playfair left them no time in which to enjoy the polite remarks of the Americans. He was forever on their backs and hurried them on with feverish activity, the cause of which *The Dolphin*'s sailors did not suspect.

Three days later, on 18 January, the first bales of cotton began to pile up in the hold. Although James Playfair no longer cared about it, the house of Playfair and Co. did excellent business, having obtained all the cotton that cluttered up Charleston's wharfs for next to nothing.

They had, however, had no further news of Crockston.

Though she said nothing, Jenny was prey to incessant fears. Her face spoke for her, altered as it was by worry, and James Playfair reassured her with kind words.

'I have every confidence in Crockston,' he said to her. 'He is a devoted servant. You who know him better than I, Miss Jenny, you should feel completely reassured. In three days your father will press you to his heart, believe me.'

'Oh, Mr James!' cried the young girl. 'How will I ever be able to acknowledge such devotion? How will my father and I find a way to repay you?'

'I will tell you when we are in British waters!' replied the young captain.

Jenny looked at him for a moment, lowered her eyes which filled with tears, and then returned to her cabin.

James Playfair hoped that the young girl would know nothing of her father's terrible situation until such time as he was safe. But during this final day, a sailor's involuntary indiscretion revealed the truth to her. The response from the Richmond cabinet had arrived the day before via a courier who had succeeded in running the line of the outposts. This response contained the verdict of death for Jonathon Halliburtt. This unfortunate citizen was to be shot by firing squad next morning. It was not long before news of the imminent execution spread through the city, and it was brought on board by one of The Dolphin's sailors. This man informed his captain of it without suspecting that Miss Halliburtt was able to hear him. The young girl gave a heartrending cry and fell unconscious to the deck. James Playfair carried her to her cabin, and the most assiduous care was required to bring her back to life.

When she opened her eyes, she saw the young captain

who, finger to his lips, counselled absolute silence. She had the strength to remain quiet and to contain the transports of her grief. James Playfair, bending down to her ear, said to her:

'Jenny, in two hours your father will be safe with you or I will have perished trying to save him!'

Then he left the poop deck, saying to himself:

'And now we have to take him at any price, even if I have to pay for his freedom with my life and with those of my entire crew!'

The time for action had arrived. Since the morning, *The Dolphin*'s cotton had been loaded in its entirety and her coal bunkers were full. She was able to depart in two hours. James Playfair had had her leave the North Commercial Wharf and taken into the open harbour. She was thus ready to take advantage of the tide, which should be in at nine o'clock in the evening.

When James Playfair left the young girl it was seven o'clock and he commenced his preparations for departure. Until then, the secret had been kept strictly between himself, Crockston and Jenny. However, he now judged it appropriate to tell Mr Mathew about the situation, and he did so that very instant.

'Yes, captain,' replied Mr Mathew without making the slightest observation. 'And this is for nine o'clock?'

'For nine o'clock. Have the fires lit immediately and have them fully stoked up.'

'It will be done, captain.'

'*The Dolphin* is lying on a kedge anchor. We will cut our rope and sail away without wasting a second.'

'Certainly.'

'Have a lantern placed at the top of the large mast. The

night is dark and the fog is lifting. We must not run the risk of losing our way when returning on board. You will even take the precaution of having the bell rung from nine o'clock.'

'Your orders will be executed punctually, captain.'

'And now, Mr Mathew,' added James Playfair, 'have the gig[14] readied. Find six of our sturdiest oarsmen. I'm going to leave immediately for White Point. I commend Miss Jenny to you during my absence and may God protect us, Mr Mathew.'

'May God protect us!' replied the first mate.

He then immediately gave the necessary orders to have the furnaces lit and the small boat readied. The latter was done in a few minutes. James Playfair, after saying one last goodbye to Miss Jenny, climbed down into his gig from where, as they pushed off, he saw torrents of black smoke vanishing into the dark fog of the sky.

It was pitch black and the wind had fallen. Absolute silence reigned over the immense harbour whose waves seemed to have been lulled. Several barely distinct lights flickered in the fog. James Playfair had taken the helm and, with a steady hand, directed his boat towards White Point at a distance of around two nautical miles. During the day, James had established his bearings perfectly and was able to gain Charleston's point in a straight line.

Eight o'clock rang out at Saint Philip's when the gig's bow struck White Point.[15]

There was still one hour to wait before the precise moment fixed by Crockston. The quay was completely deserted. Only the sentinel from the south and east battery was walking at 20 paces. James Playfair devoured the minutes. His impatience did not help to make the time pass.

At half past eight he heard the sound of footsteps. He had his men ready their oars for departure and advanced, but after ten steps he met a patrol of coastguards; there were 20 or so men in all. James drew a revolver from his belt, determined to use it if necessary. But what could he do against these soldiers who descended to the quay?

There, the head of the patrol approached him and, seeing the gig, said to James:

'What boat is this?'

'*The Dolphin*'s gig,' responded the young man.

'And you are...?'

'Captain James Playfair.'

'I thought you had left and were already in Charleston's channels.'

'I am ready to leave...I should be on my way...but...'

'But...?' asked the head of the coastguards insistently.

A sudden thought crossed James Playfair's mind and he responded:

'One of my sailors is locked up in the citadel and, well, I almost forgot him. Luckily I thought of him while there was still time and I have sent some men to get him.'

'Ah, that bad sort that you want to take back to Britain?'

'Yes.'

'We would have hung him just as well here!' said the coastguard, laughing at his joke.

'I'm sure of it,' replied James Playfair, 'but it's better for things to happen properly.'

'Good luck then, captain, and beware of the batteries on Morris Island.'

'Don't worry. As I got through without mishap, I hope to leave in the same way.'

'Mr Halliburtt?'

'Have a good journey.'

'Thank you.'

Upon this, the small troop went away and the shore remained silent.

At that moment, it struck nine o'clock. It was the appointed time. James felt his heart beating in his chest as if about to burst. A whistle rang out. James responded with a similar whistle and then waited, listening, urging his sailors to remain absolutely silent with a move of his hand. A man appeared, wrapped in a loose-fitting tartan cloak and looking here and there. James ran to him.

'Mr Halliburtt?'

'That's me,' replied the tartan-clad man.

'Oh, thank God!' exclaimed James Playfair. 'Get on board without a moment's delay. Where's Crockston?'

'Crockston!' said Mr Halliburtt in an astounded voice. 'What do you mean?'

'The man who freed you and who led you here is your servant Crockston.'

'The man who accompanied me is the gaoler from the citadel,' replied Mr Halliburtt.

'The gaoler!' cried James Playfair.

He was evidently baffled and a thousand fears assailed him.

'Ah yes, the gaoler!' exclaimed a familiar voice. 'The gaoler! He's sleeping like a log in my dungeon!'

'Crockston! You! It's you!' said Mr Halliburtt.

'Master, don't say a thing. We will explain everything to you. Your life was at stake. Get on board, get on board.'

The three men took seats in the boat.

'Push off!' cried the captain.

The six oars at once fell into their rowlocks.

'Ready all, row!' ordered James Playfair.

And the gig glided over the sombre waves of Charleston Harbour like a fish.

9

In the Crossfire

PROPELLED BY SIX STRONG oarsmen, the gig flew over the waters of the harbour. The fog was thickening, and it was not without some difficulty that James Playfair managed to keep to his bearings. Crockston had positioned himself in the bow of the boat, while Mr Halliburtt sat in the stern close to the captain. The prisoner, struck dumb at first by the presence of his servant, had attempted to speak to him, but the latter had gestured to him to remain silent.

However, when the gig was out in the open harbour a few minutes later, Crockston decided to speak. He was well aware of the questions that must have been crowding Mr Halliburtt's mind.

'Yes, my dear master,' he said, 'the gaoler has taken my place in the dungeon. I gave him two good punches as a narcotic when he was bringing me my dinner, one on the back of the neck and the other in the stomach. What gratitude! I took his clothes, I took his keys and then I went looking for you. I led you from the citadel under the soldiers' noses. It was as simple as that!'

'And my daughter?' asked Mr Halliburtt.

'On board the ship that is going to take us to Britain.'

'There! My daughter is there!' cried the American leaping from his seat.

'Silence!' replied Crockston. 'A few more minutes and we'll be safe.'

The boat flew through the darkness, but its movement was a little aimless. James Playfair was unable to make out *The Dolphin*'s lanterns in the midst of the fog. He hesitated about which direction to take; the darkness was so profound that the oarsmen were not even able to see the tips of their oars.

'Well, Mr James?' said Crockston.

'We must have done more than one and a half nautical miles,' replied the captain. 'You don't see anything, Crockston?'

'Nothing. My eyes are good as well. But we'll get there! They don't suspect anything over there...'

He had not finished speaking when a rocket streaked through the darkness and exploded at a prodigious height.

'A signal!' cried James Playfair.

'What the devil!' said Crockston. 'It must have come from the citadel. Let's wait.'

A second and then a third rocket shot upwards in the direction of the first, and almost immediately the same signal was repeated one nautical mile ahead of the boat.

'It's coming from Fort Sumter,' cried Crockston, 'and it's the escape signal. Step on your oars! They've discovered everything.'

'Pull hard, lads,' exclaimed James Playfair, rousing his sailors. 'Those rockets lit up the route. *The Dolphin* is not 800 yards away. There, I hear the bell on board. Go to it! Go to it! Twenty pounds for you if we're back in five minutes.'

The sailors propelled the gig forwards, and it seemed to skim over the waves. Everyone's heart was beating. A cannon

Jenny fell into her father's arms

shot rang out in the direction of the city and, 20 fathoms from the boat, Crockston heard rather than saw a rapid object that could well be a cannonball.

At that moment, *The Dolphin*'s bell rang out at full force. They were getting closer. A few more strokes and the boat drew alongside her. A few more seconds and Jenny fell into her father's arms.

As soon as the gig had been lifted, James Playfair rushed onto the poop deck.

'Mr Mathew, are we at pressure?'

'Yes, captain.'

'Have the painter cut and full steam ahead.'

A few moments later, the two screws propelled the steamer towards the main channel, moving her away from Fort Sumter.

'Mr Mathew,' said James, 'we cannot think of taking the Sullivan's Island channel; we would come under fire from the Confederates directly. Sail as close as possible to the right side of the harbour, even if it means a torrent from the Federal batteries. Do you have a reliable man at the helm?'

'Yes, captain.'

'Have your lanterns and the lights on board put out. The flash of the engine alone is far too much, but that cannot be helped.'

During this conversation, *The Dolphin* was moving extremely quickly, but whilst manoeuvring towards the right side of Charleston Harbour, she had been forced to follow a channel that brought her momentarily closer to Fort Sumter, and she was not half a nautical mile away when all of the fort's embrasures lit up at once and a storm of fire passed in front of the steamer with a terrible explosion.

'Too early, you oafs!' cried James Playfair, bursting into laughter. 'Faster, engineer! Faster! We have to sail between two volleys!'

The stokers stoked the furnaces and *The Dolphin*'s frame shuddered under her engine's efforts as though on the verge of falling to pieces.

At that moment, a second explosion was heard and a new shower of projectiles whistled by to the rear of the steamer.

'Too late, imbeciles!' cried the young captain with a veritable roar.

Crockston appeared on the poop deck, crying:

'One down. A few more minutes and we'll have finished with the Confederates.'

'So you think we have no more to fear from Fort Sumter?' asked James.

'No, nothing, though everything from Fort Moultrie at the tip of Sullivan's Island, but it will only be able to catch us for half a minute. It will have to choose its moment well and aim accurately if it wants to hit us. We're getting close.'

'Good! The position of Fort Moultrie will allow us to head straight into the main channel. Fire then! Fire!'

At that moment, as if James Playfair had ordered the volley himself, the fort lit up with three lines of flashes. A terrible din was heard, followed by cracks on board the steamer.

'Hit this time!' said Crockston.

'Mr Mathew,' shouted the captain to his first mate who was stationed at the bow, 'what was it?'

'The bowsprit's boom falling into the sea.'

'Are there any casualties?'

'No, captain.'

'Well, the devil take the mast! Straight into the channel! Straight! And head for the island.'

'That's the Southerners beaten!' cried Crockston. 'And if we have to be riddled with cannonballs, I'd prefer them to come from the North. It's easier to digest!'

Indeed, all danger was not averted and *The Dolphin* could not yet consider herself as having made it through. Though Morris Island was not armed with those formidable pieces that were installed a few months later, nevertheless its cannons and its mortar could easily sink a ship like *The Dolphin*.

The Federals on the island and the blockade ships had been alerted by the fire from Fort Sumter and Fort Moultrie. The besieging troops were unable to understand this night-time attack, which did not seem to be directed against themselves, but they had to remain in position and they readied themselves to respond.

James Playfair was reflecting on this very subject while they advanced down the channels of Morris Island, and he was right to be worried as, after a quarter of an hour, the darkness was criss-crossed with lights and a shower of small bombs fell around the steamer, causing water to shoot up over its rail. A few even struck *The Dolphin*'s deck, though with their base, which saved the ship from certain loss. In fact, as they learnt later, these bombs were meant to explode into a hundred fragments and cover an area of one hundred and twenty square feet with a fire that nothing could put out and that burned for 20 minutes.[16] Just one of these bombs could set a ship alight. Luckily for *The Dolphin*, they were a new invention and still extremely imperfect.

Once launched in the air, an incorrect rotational movement kept them at an angle and they fell on their bases instead of striking with their point where the percussion device was found. This construction error alone saved *The Dolphin* from certain loss. The falling of these lightweight bombs failed to cause her any great harm and, under the pressure of her superheated steam, she continued to advance down the channel.

At that moment and despite the captain's orders, Mr Halliburtt and his daughter joined James Playfair on the poop deck. The latter attempted to make them return to their cabin, but Jenny declared that she would remain with the captain.

As for Mr Halliburtt, who had just discovered the whole of his saviour's noble conduct, he shook his hand without being able to say a word.

The Dolphin advanced with great rapidity towards the open ocean. She only had to follow the channel for another three nautical miles to reach the waters of the Atlantic. If the entrance to the channel was free, she was safe. James Playfair was perfectly well aware of all of the secrets of Charleston Bay and he manoeuvred his ship in the darkness with incomparable steadiness. He thus had every reason to believe in the success of his audacious actions when a sailor on the forecastle exclaimed:

'A ship!'

'A ship?' cried James.

'Yes, on the port quarter.'

The fog, which had lifted, allowed them to make out a large frigate that was manoeuvring to close the channel and block *The Dolphin*'s passage. They had to beat her for speed at any cost and demand additional momentum from the steamer's engine. If not, all was lost.

'The helm to starboard! Full steam ahead!' shouted the captain.

He then rushed onto the bridge above the engine. Upon his orders, one of the screws was checked and, under the influence of one alone, *The Dolphin* sailed with tremendous rapidity in a circle with a very short radius as if she had turned upon herself. She thus avoided running into the Federal frigate, which was likewise advancing towards the entrance to the channel. It was now a question of speed.

James Playfair knew that there lay his salvation, alongside that of Miss Jenny and of her father and of his entire crew. The frigate had a fairly considerable lead over *The Dolphin*. It was apparent from the torrents of black smoke that were escaping from her funnel that she was stoking her fires. James Playfair was not a man to lag behind.

'Where are you at?' he shouted to the engineer.

'Maximum pressure,' replied the latter, 'steam is escaping from all the valves.'

'Charge the valves,' ordered the captain.

His orders were executed at the risk of making the vessel explode.

The Dolphin began to move faster; the piston strokes followed on from one another with terrible haste. All of the engine's base plates shook under these rapid strokes. It was a spectacle that would have made even the hardest of hearts quiver.

'Harder!' shouted James Playfair, 'Harder!'

'Impossible!' replied the engineer quickly. 'The valves are hermetically sealed. Our furnaces are jam-packed.'

'It doesn't matter! Stuff them with cotton soaked with alcohol! We have to get ahead of this blasted frigate at any cost!'

At these words, the most intrepid of the sailors looked at one another, but they did not hesitate. Several bales of cotton were thrown into the engine chamber. A barrel of alcohol was staved in, and this combustible matter was inserted into the incandescent fireboxes, not without some danger. The roaring of the flames meant that the stokers were no longer able to hear one another. The furnaces' plates were soon glowing white-hot; the pistons were coming and going like locomotive pistons; the gauges indicated a terrible pressure; the steamer flew over the waves; her joints creaked; her funnel threw out torrents of flames mixed with swirls of smoke. She was moving at a crazy, frightening speed, but she was gaining on the frigate. She overtook her; she outran her, and after ten minutes she was out of the channel.

'Safe!' exclaimed the captain.

'Safe!' replied the crew, clapping their hands.

Charleston's lighthouse was already starting to disappear to the south-west, the blaze of its lights[17] paling, and they might have thought themselves out of all danger when a bomb, launched from a gunboat that was cruising in the open sea, soared up into the darkness with a whistle. It was easy to follow its course thanks to its fuse, which left a trail of light behind it.

It is impossible to depict that moment of anxiety. Everyone fell silent, and they all watched the parabola traced by the projectile in alarm. They could do nothing to avoid it and half a minute later it fell onto The Dolphin's bow with a terrible din.

He took the bomb

The terrified sailors surged backwards to the stern; no-body dared take a step while the fuse burned with an intense crackle.

Only one brave soul ran towards this formidable instrument of destruction. It was Crockston. He took the bomb in his strong arms while thousands of sparks escaped from its fuse. Then, with superhuman effort, he threw it overboard.

The bomb had barely reached the surface of the water when there was a terrible explosion.

'Hurrah! Hurrah!' cried the whole of *The Dolphin*'s crew with one voice, while Crockston rubbed his hands.

Some time later, *The Dolphin* was cleaving through the waters of the Atlantic Ocean. The American coast disappeared into the darkness, and the distant lights that cut across one another on the horizon indicated a battle between the batteries of Morris Island and the forts of Charleston Harbour.

10

Saint Mungo

BY SUNRISE THE NEXT day, the American coast had disappeared. Not a single ship was visible on the horizon, and *The Dolphin*, reducing her terrible speed, headed at a more tranquil pace towards the Bermudas.

It is not worth recounting the crossing of the Atlantic. The return journey was not marked with a single incident, and ten days after leaving Charleston they saw the Irish coast.

What happened between the young captain and the young girl that was not foreseen, even by the least clear-sighted of people? How could Mr Halliburtt acknowledge the devotion and the courage of his saviour if not by making him the happiest of men? James Playfair did not wait until they were back in British waters to declare the feelings with which his heart was overflowing to the father and young girl, and, if Crockston is to be believed, Miss Jenny did not attempt to conceal her happiness at this confession.

Thus it was that, on 14 February of the present year, a vast crowd was gathered beneath the great vaults of Saint Mungo, Glasgow's old cathedral. Sailors, merchants, industrialists and magistrates were all present. Crockston served as witness to Miss Jenny in her bridal gown, and the worthy man was resplendent in an apple-green suit with gold buttons. A proud Uncle Vincent stood close to his nephew.

'Well, Uncle Vincent?'

In short, they were celebrating the marriage of James Playfair of Vincent Playfair and Co. of Glasgow with Miss Jenny Halliburtt of Boston.

The ceremony took place with great pomp. Everyone was aware of *The Dolphin*'s story and everyone thought the young captain's devotion justly rewarded. He alone said that he had received more than his due.

In the evening there was a grand party hosted by Uncle Vincent, with a grand meal, grand ball and a grand distribution of shillings to the crowd gathered in Gordon Street. During this memorable feast, Crockston showed marvellous voracity, though he kept within proper limits.

Everyone was happy about the marriage, some about their own happiness and others about that of other people – which is not always true of ceremonies of this type.

In the evening, when the crowd of guests had left, James Playfair embraced his uncle on both cheeks.

'Well, Uncle Vincent?' he said to him.

'Well, nephew?'

'Are you happy with the charming cargo that I brought back on board *The Dolphin*?' resumed Captain Playfair, pointing to his valiant young wife.

'Rather!' replied the worthy merchant. 'I've sold my cotton at a 375 per cent profit!'

The Geographical and Historical Context of *The Blockade Runners*
by Professor Ian Thompson

JULES GABRIEL VERNE was born on 8 February 1828 in the city of Nantes, an important port at the head of the Loire estuary. His father was a successful lawyer and it was his hope that Jules would eventually join the practice. In fact nothing could have been further from his son's mind, for he was determined to pursue a literary career and become a famous author. After completing his school studies Verne embarked on a law degree in Paris but in fact spent most of his time with a coterie of young men on the fringe of the cultural scene. In particular he became involved in the theatre and wrote libretti for operettas, a popular style of entertainment at the time. He completed his law degree, but to the frustration of his parents, persisted with his literary ambitions in Paris. Financially insecure, his situation improved when he married a young widow with two children from a bourgeois family in Amiens in northern France.

Although Verne is often referred to as 'the father of science fiction', a relatively small part of his massive output is in this vein and he had been educated in the classics rather than science. Three passions dominated his creative life: music, geography and the sea. He was an accomplished musician and on his first visit to Scotland Verne was accompanied by an old school friend, Aristide Hignard, who made his career as a musician in Paris. Verne had been fascinated by geography since his school days and his enthusiasm extended to all aspects of the environment and society. He was excited by the reports of explorers in exotic lands and indeed came to describe his writings as being 'geographical novels'. He became a member of *La Société de Géographie de Paris*, the world's oldest geographical society, and his world famous series of over 60 novels became known as *Les Voyages Extraordinaires*. He drew on his geographical reading to set his adventures in exotic countries and in every environment from arctic cold to arid deserts and lush tropical forests. Though the plots are sometimes a little unlikely, they are situated in authentic, carefully researched, settings. In an interview with Marie Belloc in 1895, Verne explained:

> I have always been devoted to the study of Geography, much as some people delight in history and historical research. I really think that my love of maps and the great explorers led to my composing the first of my long series of geographical stories.

Verne's passion for the sea and sailing stemmed from his childhood. The Verne family never lived far from the River Loire and also acquired a summer holiday house overlooking the port. Verne was exposed to a bustling port trading in exotic products from romantic-sounding far distant colonies. The spectacle of shipping was further enhanced by the clamour of heavy industries associated with ship building and repairing. Indeed, Verne's passion for the sea was used to perpetrate a myth that as a child he smuggled himself aboard a vessel headed abroad from Nantes, and had to be intercepted by his father further downstream. Verne himself denied the veracity of this invention. His enthusiasm for sailing later materialised in the purchase of three vessels, each one larger and more luxurious than its predecessor as his wealth increased.

In addition to these three passions, Verne had a further emotional attachment. He claimed Scottish ancestry on his mother's side from a 15th century Scot, Allott, who had enlisted in the Scottish regiment of King Louis XI of France. After loyal service he was ennobled and assumed the name of Allotte de la Fuÿe, signifying the right to own a dovecote on his property. From boyhood Verne had revelled in this Scottish connection, which was further enhanced by his admiration of the works of Sir Walter Scott, whose complete works he had read in translation. As he said to Marie Belloc:

> All my life I have delighted in the works of Sir Walter Scott, and during a never-to-be-forgotten tour in the British Isles, my happiest days were spent in Scotland. I can still see, as in a vision, beautiful picturesque Edinburgh with its Heart of Midlothian, and many entrancing memories; the Highlands, world-forgotten Iona, and the wild Hebrides. Of course to one familiar with the works of Scott, there is scarce a district of his native land lacking some association with the writer and his immortal work.

The 1859 visit to Scotland

It was Verne's first visit to Scotland in 1859 that provided him with the local knowledge of Glasgow and the Clyde which was to be the launch pad for *The Blockade Runners*.

On Friday 26 August 1859, at the age of 31, Verne set foot for the first time on his beloved Scotland. His visit had been made possible by his travelling companion Aristide Hignard whose brother, a shipping agent, had offered them free passage on a cargo vessel to Liverpool. Verne was astonished by the scale of activity in the port, but this was not his destination. The following afternoon the two friends set off by train to Edinburgh, arriving in pouring rain at midnight. From their base in a hotel on Princes Street they explored Edinburgh, and were particularly excited by the Old Town and its connection with Scott's *The Heart of Midlothian*. From the summit of Arthur's Seat, Verne witnessed a panorama of the city and the Firth of Forth that was to remain long in his memory. Edinburgh was also to provide him with rare contact with a Scottish family. Hignard's brother had married the niece of a Scottish businessman, William Bain, at that time manager of the Edinburgh branch of the City of Glasgow Bank. The two companions visited the Bain household on Inverleith Row in the New Town. Here they met two crucial people, both of whom could speak French. Margaret Bain, the eldest daughter, assisted Verne by providing him with an itinerary to fulfil his most earnest wish – to visit the Highlands in the short time available. Secondly, a dinner guest, the Catholic priest William Smith (later to become the Archbishop of Edinburgh), invited the two Frenchmen to visit him at his brother's baronial mansion in Fife en route to Glasgow.

Accordingly, on 29 August Verne and Hignard boarded the steamer *The Prince of Wales* at Granton Harbour and headed up the Firth of Forth in the teeth of a gale and driving rain. With great difficulty, the two men were put ashore by dinghy at Crombie Point on the Fife coast where they were met by the Reverend Mr Smith. After a warming tot of whisky at the local tavern they walked across the fields to his brother's mansion, Inzievar House, a newly completed baronial edifice in magnificent grounds, decorated with priceless works of art. After a gargantuan lunch, the journey continued by train via Stirling to Glasgow. Exiting from Queen Street Station, the two friends emerged on to George Square and took a room in the Royal Hotel. After the usual supper of cold meat washed down with ale, Verne and Hignard explored Glasgow by night. Reaching the Clyde, Verne's first impression was that the harbour was less spectacular than Liverpool, clearly being a river port rather than a seaport. Exhausted after a tiring journey, the pair deferred further exploration of the city until the following morning. The rain continued the next day as the friends made their way eastwards, straddling open filthy streams, to the old nucleus of the city. Here Verne found that access to the cathedral was closed and the adjacent necropolis depressed him. After this inauspicious start, Verne took shelter in a cab and ordered the coachman to drive them through the city centre. At once Verne's impressions of the city improved. Probably following the Trongate and passing the Tontine Hotel, Verne admired the handsome civic and commercial buildings. As the cab followed the waterfront he realised the immense value of the cargo being handled by the port. Continuing downstream he traversed the shipyards and factories between the Broomielaw Quay and Partick, which was to be the setting of the construction of *The Dolphin*. Having witnessed the frenetic activity on both banks of the Clyde, the cab crossed the newly established

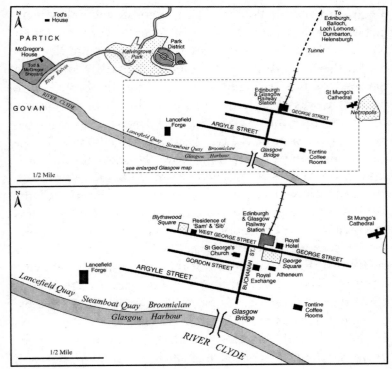

Jules Verne's Glasgow
Cartography by Mike Shand

Kelvingrove Park and via the bourgeois districts of Park and Blythswood Square to regain George Square. After a hurried lunch, Verne and Hignard left Glasgow by train for Loch Lomond. This section of the journey was not without significance. The railway followed the north shore of the Clyde and, sitting in an open carriage despite the rain, Verne was afforded a clear view of the channel marked by stone piers which were to guide *The Dolphin* to the open sea.

Verne's first visit to Scotland continued via Loch Lomond,

The Trossachs and 'Stirling, back to Edinburgh and then by overnight train to London. The details of this section of the journey are not relevant to this present discussion but were exploited in two of Verne's other 'Scottish' novels, *The Children of Captain Grant* and *The Underground City*.

What had Verne experienced relative to *The Blockade Runners* apart from his general exposure to Scotland and the excitement that this generated? He had discovered that Edinburgh and Glasgow were two very different cities. While Edinburgh had architectural glories, a spectacular setting, a patrician bourgeoisie as well as immense historical and literary importance, it nevertheless had a horribly deprived underclass in parts of the Old Town; Glasgow was a product of the industrial revolution and transatlantic trading. The development of industry and commerce in Glasgow was sustained by influxes of workers from the Highlands and Ireland, producing overcrowded housing and a growing disparity between a wealthy commercial class and a poor, if semi-skilled, working class who at least had access to employment. How much of this complex social structure Verne absorbed in such a short visit to Glasgow can be doubted, but he had grasped the essential point that the city and its maritime connections afforded better literary potential for a marine adventure story than Edinburgh. Above all, as compared with the sedate atmosphere of Edinburgh, at least in the New Town, he had realised that along the banks of the Clyde, Glasgow was a city of noise; of hammers against metal, of timber being sawn and of ships sirens. This affront to the senses is clearly conveyed in *The Blockade Runners* until *The Dolphin* is far out to sea and the sound of gunfire takes over from the noise of construction.

The manuscript and publication of The Blockade Runners

Verne's visit to Glasgow in 1859 in part provided the inspiration for *The Blockade Runners*. At this time he had seen most of the sites mentioned in the novella. He had seen Glasgow Cathedral, the scene of the marriage of Jenny and James Playfair, albeit only from the exterior. He had passed the Tontine Hotel where the Playfairs had hatched their plot and had followed the Clyde Harbour as far as Partick where the shipyard of Tod and McGregor was located. Moreover, on his journey to Loch Lomond the train had followed the Clyde as far as Dumbarton. He had not witnessed a launch from the Clyde shipyards, but from an almost identical situation in the Loire yards at Nantes, he was fully aware of the technique of launching into a narrow river using restraining chains to prevent a collision with the opposite bank.

The story closes before the end of the Civil War – the triumph of the North and the recapture of Charleston. In fact, the novella was penned before the end of hostilities, which in Charleston's case was February 1865 when Fort Sumter was retaken and the city, now reduced to ruins through bombardment, surrendered. The term 'Civil War' is considered inappropriate and pejorative by some American scholars in the sense that it was not an attempt to overthrow a national government. Alternative titles such as 'The War between the States' or 'The War of Secession' are preferred by some. Despite this, the designation of 'Civil War' still has the widest currency, including in recent books published in Charleston and official guides such as those published by the National Parks authority, and is therefore used here.

The novella was first published in the *Musée des familles: lectures du soir* in two instalments in October and November 1865. It was reprinted in July 1871 by Verne's publisher, Hetzel, in small page format, and with some revisions in the series *Magasin d'Education et de Récréation*. As a short novella, it was insufficiently long to publish as a single volume and accompanied a longer novel, *Une Ville flottante*, based on Verne's voyage with his brother Paul from Liverpool to New York aboard the *Great Eastern* liner. In 1872, it was republished in a hardback octavo edition in the *Voyages Extraordinaires* series with multicoloured covers much prized by bibliophiles. This is the edition which has been used in the present translation. The revised hand-written manuscript showing Verne's corrections is now in the possession of the Municipal Library at Nantes and is housed in a special collection at the *Centre d'etudes verniennes*. The first page of the manuscript can be viewed online via the website www.nantes.fr/julesverne by following the link *Les Collections*.

The slavery question

Jules Verne displays an ambiguous attitude to the slave issue in *The Blockade Runners*, even though the animated discussions between James Playfair and Jenny indicate his full awareness of the moral issues. With his voracious appetite for reading and his inquiring mind, it is inconceivable that Verne was not aware from a young age that the early wealth of his home city of Nantes was intimately linked to the slave trade. Indeed, the handsome mansions lining the north bank of the Loire were testament to the success of the slavers' trade. Wealth was generated not only from the sale of slaves to the plantation owners of the French Caribbean and Indian Ocean, but also from the import of coffee, sugar, cotton and spices. Moreover, profit was made from the related activities of shipbuilding, rope and sail making, food processing and the business involved in banking and insurance. The fact that he did not venture deeply into the slavery issue at the early stages of his literary career probably reflects the delicacy of the question at that time. Nantes had been France's foremost slaving port and to have explicitly evoked the undoubted cruelty of the trade would not have been appreciated by his readership. Consequently, Verne treads warily through this moral minefield and allows the debate to be conducted through the surrogate voices of Jenny and James. Instead, his narrative concentrates on naval and military matters and on the economic disruption caused by the Civil War. It has been suggested that Verne's antipathy to the secession of the Southern States owed more to his fear of the breakup of the Union rather than to an opposition to the slave system. However, it is clear from the later novels, *Un Capitaine de quinze ans* (1878) and *Nord contre Sud* (1887) that Verne came to detest slavery and if the problem is somewhat muted in *The Blockade Runners* we can consider that he was inspired to write an exciting maritime adventure rather than to adopt a moral stance.

Glasgow at the time of The Blockade Runners

At the time of the fictitious launch of *The Dolphin* in December 1862, Glasgow was still much as Verne had seen it in 1859, albeit with an enlarged population and economy. The city was one with two faces. At one extreme, the working population endured poor and overcrowded housing in the east of the city and along the banks of the Clyde. The resulting prevalence of bad sanitation and disease had at least been alleviated by the arrival of clean water from Verne's favourite loch, Loch Katrine, in the year of Verne's visit. At the other extreme, handsome squares, churches and public buildings graced the city centre. Impressive mansions and terraces owned by the city's industrialists and businessmen burgeoned in the new suburbs to the west and south of the city centre, where the prevailing westerly winds drove away the fumes and pollution. This spatial segregation was also reflected in the extremes of the social structure. The working class, swollen by the immigration of job seekers from Ireland and the Scottish Highlands, suffered not only the grime and noise of their streets and workplaces, but also the ardours of physical labour, long working hours and limited holiday time. By contrast, the bourgeoisie enjoyed spacious properties, often with resident servants and, in the case of the most affluent, private transport in the form of coaches. While the poorest class had little time or resources for leisure activity beyond church attendance, the rich could afford a fine lifestyle and social involvement in, for example, exclusive men's clubs. Nevertheless, one territory was common to all classes. The city's fine parks and botanic gardens were shared spaces enjoyed by all citizens and Verne saw one of the largest and finest, Kelvingrove Park, in the city's West End.

This view of a city harshly divided by class is exaggerated and simplified, but Verne was to see elements of the extremes in the squalor of the old nucleus south of the cathedral, especially compared to the comfort and privacy of the Coffee Room of the Tontine Hotel.

The plot of the novella depends upon a blend of political, marine and economic geography that was solidly based on reality. From being essentially a market and ecclesiastical town, the industrial revolution transformed Glasgow into a powerhouse of both manufacturing and maritime trade. Although Verne focuses on the crisis in the textile industry brought about by the disruption of the import of raw cotton, in fact, by the 1850s, Glasgow had an incredibly diverse manufacturing base, ranging from heavy locomotives at

The Merchant City – Glasgow's link with the tobacco trade

one end of the scale to engineering components and timber working at the other. Glasgow and its Clydeside hinterland could thus provide many products lacking in the American South due to the Federal blockade, and thanks to the improvement of navigation on the river and estuary, Glasgow's manufacturers had the capacity to trade in bulk across the Atlantic. In practice, Verne focuses on the two key industries that were essential for his plot. Firstly, textile manufacture was a major industry in Clydeside, launched using water power but modernised and expanded by the introduction of steam-driven machinery. By 1860, over 200,000 people were employed in the sector which produced high value muslins and embroidered cloth. The cotton magnates were well aware of the fate of the 'Tobacco Lords', who had lost their fortunes by being deprived of imported tobacco as a result of the American War of Independence. Consequently, they feared a similar catastrophe as a result of the Civil War if they were unable to import the life blood of their industry – raw cotton. Secondly, the Clyde had developed a shipbuilding industry and, in particular, had pioneered the use of iron in the construction of hulls. This was coupled with world-leading innovations in the design of marine steam engines to produce vessels that were both robust and speedy. Thus by the time that the blockade was installed, Glasgow had the capacity to produce vessels capable of crossing the Atlantic and of outrunning the Federal blockade ships. This was a fortuitous conjunction for the Clydeside shipyards. The demise of the construction of ships for the cotton trade was compensated by the demand for blockade running ships to export arms and other manufactured goods needed in the under-industrialised South, now separated from the more developed North, and to return to Britain with cargoes of cotton. Shipbuilding had burgeoned and by the outbreak of the Civil War over 20 shipyards lined the Clyde between Glasgow and Port Glasgow, with Clydeside producing half of Britain's ship tonnage. Unsurprisingly, agents from both North and South were present in Glasgow to monitor shipbuilding activity. It is impossible to put an appropriate figure on the size of the workforce, since in addition to the actual construction in the yards, companies provided engines, boilers, brass and copper components, sail cloth, rigging ropes and timber. The internal fitting out of vessels was often lavish and required skill in design and craftwork. As construction evolved from sail to a combination of steam and sail, and from timber to

An extract from Tod and McGregor's ship list. The ships *Jupiter*, *Alliance*, *Spunkie*, *Kelpie* and *Princess Royal* were blockade runners.

Courtesy of Glasgow University Business Archives

a composite of timber covering an iron frame, and eventually to iron ships, the range of skills required to complete a ship progressively widened. The clamour of metal beating and timber cutting that Verne evokes was just the more obvious manifestation of an industry dependent on a wide range of skills and talent extending well beyond the yards themselves. An analysis of all of the 1862 copies of Glasgow's leading daily newspaper, *The Glasgow Herald*, reveals three major preoccupations. First and foremost was the conduct of the war itself. Reports on the evolution of the war were carried virtually daily and covered the battles, often in gruesome detail. The accounts were frequently spread over an entire five-column broadsheet page. Secondly, the crisis in the cotton textile industry was often described, usually accompanied by statistics on the reduction of imported bales and the number of unemployed and partially unemployed workers, not only in the Glasgow area but also in England's major cotton textiles industry areas in Lancashire. Letters to the Editor described the paucity of alternative sources, especially from India, where the inadequacy of local transport systems limited the volume of cotton that could be exported. Moreover, the European demand for raw cotton had pushed up prices to the extent that it was more profitable to produce cotton goods locally in India, further deepening the crisis in Britain. Thirdly, it is clear that there was little mention in the newspaper of the involvement of the Clyde shipbuilding industry in the conflict. We must assume that this was a sensitive issue to which the press was willing to turn a blind eye to, rather than compromise a profitable industry and source of employment.

Charleston at the time of
The Blockade Runners

Charleston became known as the capital of Southern slavery, not only due to the sheer numbers involved in the trade, but also because of the degree to which the exploitation of slaves shaped the city's prosperity and development. At the height of the trade, half of the city's population was black and in the early decades of the 19th century, three-quarters of the city's households owned at least one slave. As the major slave importing port, Charleston thrived on the basis of the trade and on the systems that it sustained. Initially, the slaves fulfilled the demand for labour on the rice and cotton plantations, where their resistance to diseases resulting from the unhealthy summer climate provided a workforce that the white population could neither sustain nor wish to participate in. Over the decades, the slaves' social structure evolved considerably, in particular with a differentiation between the rural field workers on the plantations, with little or no opportunity for advancement, and the urban slaves resident in Charleston. In the city, though the slaves were deprived of fundamental rights such as education and marriage, they nevertheless could acquire trades and skills. In the hectic rice and cotton harvesting period between October and March, a large proportion of the male black population worked in the back-breaking role of stevedores (dockers) in the port. However, slaves also worked as butchers, fishmongers, barbers, carpenters, shoemakers and even firemen. Among other activities, many of the female slaves worked as domestic servants, cooks, seamstresses and market traders. The city's slaves were obliged to reside in

The fife and drum reveille.
Illustrated London News

segregated basic accommodation on their owner's property and were subject to a curfew and exclusion from fashionable parts of the city, such as the Battery overlooking Charleston Harbour. However, some were sufficiently entrepreneurial to accumulate enough savings to purchase their freedom, although they remained as second-class citizens with severe constraints on their rights. The curfew extended from nine at night until six in the morning, at which time a reveille on fife and drum signalled that slaves were allowed to leave their owner's property.

By the time that *The Dolphin* would have reached Charleston in 1862, the city's population had grown to

40,500 inhabitants of whom 23,000 were white, over 3,200 were freed slaves, and approximately 14,000 were still in slavery. This meant Charleston was the third largest city in the South as a result of the combination of slavery and related trading activity. The shore of the Cooper River was lined by 19 wharves sustaining the thriving exports of raw cotton and rice, as well as the import of manufactured goods, luxury items and increasingly after 1860, arms and ammunition. Small scale industries such as rice milling had developed on the Ashley River on the western side of the peninsula, and connections had been made with the hinterland by a new railroad. As a result, the white population was dominated by a bourgeoisie of plantation owners, shippers, the business and professional classes and property owners, who all constituted a kind of Southern 'aristocracy' devoted to high living and stylish manners. In turn, this display of indulgent wealth which was manifest in handsome mansions and participation in clubs and cultural organisations, depended on the import of luxury goods, especially from Europe, as the South lacked the appropriate industries to supply this sophisticated demand. This wealth amongst the political elite gave rise to a growing self-confidence and, in common with neighbouring slave-owning States, an increased resentment of perceived political control from a remote group of Northern States with a wholly different economic system and growing opposition to slavery.

Although the bourgeoisie constituted the critical political mass, it must not be imagined that Charleston had a simple binary composition of affluent whites and servile blacks. In fact, the social structure of the city was composed of a wide range, from wealthy plantation owners and business professionals to the underclass of an impoverished and marginalised white population, including criminals and prostitutes. Nevertheless, the impact of secession and the resultant blockade by the Northern navy threatened the survival of all social classes but none more so than the cotton producers and exporters whose activities were the backbone of the city's economy. Nevertheless, it was the political

A gentleman of leisure enjoys an after-dinner smoke in Charleston.
Illustrated London News

'deciders' who most suffered the consequences of the blockade. The reduced ability to export raw cotton severely restricted cash accumulation, while the disruption of imports deprived the city not only of arms and munitions, but also of the luxury goods which had sustained a gracious style of living.

To finance everyday living, the Confederate States created their own paper money. In effect, the Confederate Dollar was a 'national' currency and bore patriotic designs and portraits of Southern war heroes. As the cost of the war spiralled, so the value of the paper money devalued and the notes, of which over 80 million were printed, bore ever

Above:
Traditional Charleston street scene. St Philip's Church was used as a lighthouse
to guide blockade runners into the port

Below:
The Battle Fort Sumter, April 1861

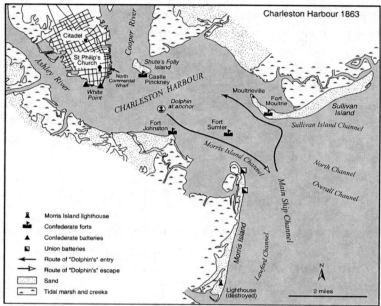

Charleston Harbour at the time of *The Blockade Runners*
Cartography by Mike Shand

higher notional value. Confederate bonds were also issued and were traded internationally, but at the cost of very high interest rates.

Charleston was captured by the Federal army after a bombardment which caused massive destruction in the city. Over the decades, the effort of reconstruction has been prodigious and the historic core has been virtually restored. Even if the resultant townscape is not totally authentic when compared with the mid-19th century town, there is nevertheless no denying that Charleston has considerable charm and any 'disneyfication' of one of America's most iconic Southern cities has been avoided. One of the most attractive features of the city, which has now grown to over

120,000 inhabitants, is that it is possible to take a boat trip down the harbour which replicates *The Dolphin*'s breaking of the blockade. The excursion route from the docks of the Cooper River to Fort Sumter passes the forts and channels mentioned in *The Blockade Runners*. The tour boats land at Fort Sumter, now a National Park, and even if the restored fort bears little resemblance to the original, its strategic location close to the mouth of Charleston Harbour is evident and evocative of the novella.

The construction of The Dolphin

In most respects, Verne's description of the construction of *The Dolphin* is an accurate representation of shipbuilding on the Clyde at the time of the Civil War. The company concerned, Tod and McGregor, existed in reality and the location at the confluence of the Kelvin and the Clyde is accurate. The name given by Verne as 'Kelvin Dock' differs from the normal name of Meadowside. The company was formed by David Tod and John McGregor in 1837, former employees of the famous Napier company, and specialised in marine engines and the construction of iron ships. The company was founded in 1837 and, after various sites close to Glasgow Harbour, moved to the more spacious site in 1844 where the confluence with the Kelvin permitted the launch of larger ships. At the time of Verne's 1859 visit, both owners had recently died, McGregor in 1858 aged 57 and Tod in 1859 aged 64. The passing of McGregor was greatly mourned in Partick, with shops closing and ships in Glasgow Harbour lowering their flags to half mast on the day of his funeral. He was buried in the necropolis adjacent

Tod and McGregor's shipyard at the height of its activity

to Glasgow Cathedral. The company constructed the first dry dock on the Clyde. McGregor resided on the site, whereas Tod lived in a villa on the hillside overlooking the river, where the steep path to the shipyard is still referred to as 'Tod's Brae', at least by older citizens. At the time of Verne's visit, the shipyard was operated by the sons of Tod and McGregor, 18 and 25 years old respectively, and the company's involvement in the construction of blockade runners was accurate, as it built 11 vessels for this purpose. None of these bore the name *Dolphin* however, which was pure invention by Verne. By contrast, the reference to *The Dolphin*'s engine as having been constructed by Lancefield Forge correctly refers to Napier's yard, manufacturers of very high quality marine steam engines. The founder, Robert Napier, was well known in France, having been awarded the *Légion d'honneur* by Napoléon III in 1855. Similarly, the mention of the engine design being developed by Dudgeon

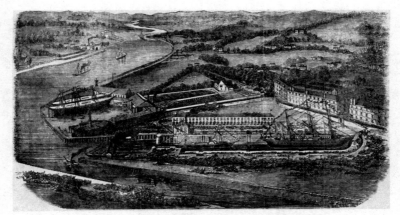

The shipyards of Tod and McGregor in Partick, Glasgow,
where *The Dolphin* was built.
Illustrated London News

of Millwall on the Isle of Dogs on the Thames is also based
on fact. Dudgeon's yard was adjacent to the shipyard of
John Russell, where Verne had witnessed the construction
of the *Leviathan* in 1859, later renamed the *Great Eastern*
on which he sailed to New York in 1867.

There is no evidence that Verne witnessed the launch of
a blockade runner on the Clyde during his very brief coach
ride along the riverside. However, from his experience of
the shipyards on the Loire at Nantes, he would have been
very familiar with the technique of launching ships stern
first down greased slipways into a narrow river, restrained
by heavy chains to prevent collision with the opposite bank.

The Dolphin's *transatlantic adventure*

The hero or, in nautical terms, the heroine of the novella, is
The Dolphin herself. Verne's knowledgeable crowd from

The Tontine Hotel where the plot to run the Charleston blockade was hatched

Partick and Govan (districts on opposite banks of the Clyde) who witnessed the launch were well aware that this was a special vessel. Although they would have been used to regular launches, nevertheless *The Dolphin* clearly had exceptional features. The shallow draught, the twin independent propellers and the evident power of the vessel marked her out as a purpose-built ship whose function as a potential blockade runner was evident. In fact throughout the tale, *The Dolphin* performed exactly as designed. Lightly armed, she relied on speed and manoeuvrability to outwit the Federal opponents, and the element of surprise was exploited to the full by her skipper to avoid capture. The rationale for *The Dolphin's* design is provided by the conversation between Vincent Playfair, an important Glasgow

The modern Tontine House, which replicates some of the facade
of the Tontine Hotel

shipping merchant, and his nephew James, a young sea
captain, held in the Coffee Room of the Tontine Hotel. A
plot is hatched which matches daring and boldness with
greed and is driven by the very survival of the Playfair
company and the parlous state of the city's textile industry.

Of all the *dramatis personae*, Crockston is perhaps the
least finely drawn by Verne. We know that he is utterly
devoted to his master, the Northern journalist Halliburtt,
and that he is possessed of immense physical strength. Nevertheless, he imagines an ingenious rescue plan but once his
mission is successfully accomplished, he fades away from
the *denouement* of the story.

By contrast, Jenny Halliburtt is portrayed by Verne in
uncharacteristically tender terms. He professed to his publisher Hetzel that he had no skill in describing the fair sex,

Verne chose Glasgow Cathedral for Jenny's wedding,
though he himself had never seen the interior

being more at home with the adventurous potential of men.
However, in the space of a few days, Jenny makes the tran-
sition from an anxious young girl to an adult willing to
commit to a future as wife to an impetuous sea captain.
Verne shows us a girl sick with anxiety for the safety of her
father imprisoned in the citadel at Charleston, but unwilling
to compromise as to the rightness of the Northern cause.
She displays bravery in refusing to desert Playfair's side
throughout the action and if she never completely converts
him to her political beliefs, she nevertheless wins his admiration and eventually his heart.

With his love of the sea and sailing, Verne is more con-
fident in his characterisation of James Playfair. He portrays
him as a flamboyant, self-confident, young man, a skilled
mariner and decisive leader whose hard-headed tempera-
ment is softened by his affection for Jenny. The plot of the

novella depends on the partnership between the technical capacity of *The Dolphin* and its skilful exploitation by James' seamanship.

The Blockade Runners is a superbly constructed novella. It commences energetically in Glasgow with the launch of *The Dolphin* and continues with dual plots – that of Vincent and James Playfair and, simultaneously, that of Crockston and Jenny. The discovery of Crockston's deception is followed by a crescendo of action as the blockade is run, Jonathan Halliburtt rescued and the blockade penetrated again. The return voyage is tranquil and followed by the joyous ending of the wedding in Glasgow Cathedral. On the surface it is a straightforward but imaginative story, based on the historical and geographical detail researched by Verne, which gives conviction to the action. Beneath the plot however, he raises issues that he finds troubling, particularly in relation to slavery. In addition, we see the early signs of Verne's antipathy towards greed and wealth accumulation, relished in *The Blockade Runners* by Vincent Playfair which was to become more dominant in his later works.

Conclusion

THE CIVIL WAR ENDED symbolically for Glasgow as the last Confederate unit to surrender was the crew of the *Shenandoah* in Liverpool in November 1865. This mighty 1,152 ton composite (wood on iron frame) vessel had been built by Stephen's yard on the Clyde, and had been launched as the *Sea King* in August 1863 as a trading vessel. In November 1864, guns were mounted and she became the Confederate cruiser *Shenandoah*. By the time of her surrender and transfer to the American Consul, she had sunk 40 Federal ships. She ended her days as a yacht and trade ship for the Sultan of Zanzibar. Thus Glasgow was involved from virtually the start to the end of the Civil War. However, Verne completes his novella before the end of the Civil War, and in fact does not refer to the carnage of the land battles in which 650,000 souls lost their lives. The crescendo of action is essentially maritime as the blockade is run not once, but twice. Thereafter the return voyage to Glasgow is peaceful and followed by a happy conclusion: the wedding of James to Jenny and the achievement of a considerable profit for the Playfair company.

Little remains in Glasgow to recall its involvement in the Civil War. The shipyard of Tod and McGregor has long since disappeared, although appropriately the confluence of the Clyde and the Kelvin is now the site of a spectacular new Transport Museum which houses the city's vast collection

The new Transport Museum close to the site of Tod and McGregor's shipyard. The museum houses exhibitions of shipbuilding on the Clyde

of maritime artifacts. Berthed alongside is the restored Clyde-built windjammer, the magnificent *Glenlee*. Roughly a kilometre to the north, in Glasgow's West End, a town house owned in the 19th century by a wealthy merchant, James Smith, who had traded with the United States and was an ardent supporter of the Confederate cause. He aided the South financially and his younger brother, a colonel in the Mississippi Rifles, died defending a railway bridge in Kentucky. Smith's support for the Confederates brought him into contact with President Jefferson Davis. Davis had been captured in May 1865 and incarcerated in Virginia. He was harshly treated and his health suffered. He was eventually released from prison as part of the general amnesty of 1868 and the following year Davis visited Scotland, where he was a guest of the Smith family. The house still stands much as he would have found it.

Jefferson Davis, defeated President of the Confederation, visited his friend
James Smith in 1869. Here he is seated outside Smith's mansion
The Mitchell Library

It is difficult today to follow *The Dolphin's* course down
the Clyde by boat. The nearest approximation is offered by
the summer schedule of the paddle steamer PS *Waverley* which
sails summer excursions from Glasgow down the Clyde to
a variety of West Coast destinations.

A more official celebration of the Civil War exists in
Edinburgh and, as in so many respects when in comparison
with Glasgow, the capital takes a contrary view of the situation. The Civil War memorial in the Old Burial Ground at
the foot of Calton Hill is unambiguously in favour of the
North. In a double statuary, a freed slave extends his arms
in gratitude to a statue of Abraham Lincoln.

Overall, we must conclude that Glasgow's involvement
in the Civil War had both positive and negative effects,
depending from which side of the Atlantic one views them.

Memorial devoted to the Scots who fought in the Union army.
The statue depicts a slave showing his gratitude to Abraham Lincoln

As seen from Glasgow, Clydeside's involvement in the construction of blockade runners and access to imported cotton brought wealth to the shipbuilders and merchants. The reprieve to the textiles industry was only partial and never led to a recovery of its past eminence as a major employer. However, the technological advances, especially in the design of the high-pressure marine engines required to deliver the speed necessary to break through the Federal blockade, ensured the future prosperity of shipbuilding on the Clyde on a world scale, which was to last until the close of the Second World War.

Viewed from across the Atlantic, the balance sheet is less favourable. The construction of blockade runners, some of which were owned and crewed by Scots, enabled the supply of arms and munitions to the Confederate army and thus, to some extent, prolonged the most bloodthirsty carnage in the history of America. In this sense, Verne's portrayal of events in *The Blockade Runners* is a less than balanced picture of the reality of the struggle. The novella must thus be viewed as a rather uncritical but stirring construction of a maritime adventure and consequently as a romance rather than as a totally accurate historical or moral commentary.

Further reading

THE VOLUME OF LITERATURE available on the American Civil War is enormous and most public and educational libraries will have substantial collections. A useful summary, well illustrated with maps and photographs, is Bruce Catton, *The Penguin Book of the American Civil War*, Penguin Books Ltd. Harmondsworth, 1966. This was first published in America by American Heritage Publishing Co. 1966.

A recent authoritative book on Glasgow's involvement is Eric J Graham, *Clyde Built: Blockade Runners, Cruisers and Armoured Rams of the American Civil War*, Berlinn, Edinburgh, 2006.

A comprehensive history of shipbuilding on the Clyde, including reference to the war, is Fred M Walker, *The Song of the Clyde: A History of Clyde Shipbuilding*, John Donald, Edinburgh, 2001.

An American account of blockade running is provided by Stephen Wise, *Lifeline of the Confederacy: Blockade Running during the American Civil War*, University of South Carolina Press, 1988.

The most evocative account of Charleston during the war is David Detzer, *Allegiance: Fort Sumter, Charleston, and the Beginning of the Civil War*, Harcourt, New York, 2001.

A compact, very well illustrated history of Charleston is Robert Rosen, *A Short History of Charleston*, Lexicos, San Francisco, 1982.

The University of Glasgow Archive Service has a comprehensive collection of the records of Clydeside companies involved in the construction of blockade runners, the titles of which can be consulted online via the university website, www.gla.ac.uk/archives, entitled *Blockade running during the American Civil War: Sources*.

For an account of Verne's visit to Scotland and the Clyde in 1859, including his stay in Glasgow, see IB Thompson, *The Visit to Scotland by Jules Verne in 1859*, Scottish Geographical Journal, vol 121, no 1, 2005.

For a more comprehensive study of Jules Verne's relationship with Scotland, including a critical essay on *The Blockade Runners*, see Ian Thompson, *Jules Verne's Scotland, In Fact and Fiction*, Luath Press, Edinburgh, 2011.

End Notes

1 The correct name was 'Meadowside', situated at the confluence of the River Kelvin with the Clyde.

2 Verne uses 'anglais' or 'English' here, as he does throughout the text. 'Scottish' or 'British' have been substituted as deemed appropriate. It is still commonplace for the French to use 'England' when referring to the whole of the United Kingdom.

3 An instrument that indicates the speed of a vessel using needles and graduated dials.

4 Seven leagues and 87/100. One nautical mile equals 1,852 metres.

5 This was a guide to good practice as a merchant written in the 15th century by Benedikt Kotruljevic. A French edition was published in 1613 entitled *The Perfect Merchant*.

6 Pillars of stone surmounted by a light.

7 A large barge used for transporting freight on rivers and estuaries.

8 Newspaper entirely devoted to the abolition of slavery.

9 5,556 metres, a little more than 5½ kilometres.

10 Name given to the stern of American vessels.

11 In fact this lighthouse had been demolished by the Confederates so as not to guide Federal vessels involved in the blockade.

12 It is on this island that the famous American novelist Edgar Allan Poe set his strangest scenes.

13 Five kilometres.

14 Light boat with pointed bow and stern.

15 St Philip's Church still stands and is one of the finest in Charleston.

16 This 'grégeois' shell was an incendiary device which could burn on water and was used in naval warfare.

17 In fact the Confederates had removed the lights so that the Federals could not reconstruct the lighthouse.

Some other books published by **LUATH** PRESS

Jules Verne's Scotland: In fact and fiction
Ian Thompson
ISBN 978 1 906817 37 4 HBK £16.99

I still see, as in a vision, beautiful picturesque Edinburgh, with its Heart of Midlothian, and many entrancing memories; the Highlands, world-forgotten Iona, and the wild Hebrides.
JULES VERNE, 1895

Jules Verne's first visit to Scotland lasted a mere five days, but that was enough to instil within him a lifelong passion for the small country; a passion which had a profound impact on his literary work and fuelled his creative imagination.

Two journeys, 20 years apart, and five novels set partly or wholly in Scotland, show how the influence of the country rippled all the way through his life. *Jules Verne's Scotland* guides the reader through Verne's journeys, first in 1859 and again in 1879, where he witnessed the majesty of Edinburgh and the industrial buzz of Glasgow together with the unspoilt beauty of the Highlands and Islands.

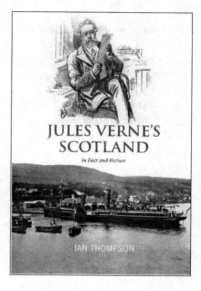

As well as providing insights into Verne's travels in Scotland, Ian Thompson provides analysis of novels such as *The Underground City* and *The Green Ray* that immortalise Scotland in their pages.

The Underground City, a novel set in Scotland
Jules Verne
Translated by Sarah Crozier, with a foreword by Professor Ian Thompson
ISBN 978 1842820 80 3 PBK £7.99

Ten years after manager James Starr left the Aberfoyle mine underneath Loch Katrine exhausted of coal, he receives an intriguing missive that suggests that the pit isn't barren after all. When Starr returns to and discovers that there is indeed more coal to quarry, he and his workers are beset by strange events, hinting at a presence that does not wish to see them excavate the cavern further.

Could there be someone out to sabotage their work? Someone with a grudge against them? Or is something more menacing afoot, something supernatural that they cannot see or understand? When one of his miners falls in love with a young girl found abandoned down a mineshaft, their unknown assailant makes it clear that nothing will stop its efforts to shut down the mine, even if it means draining Loch Katrine itself!

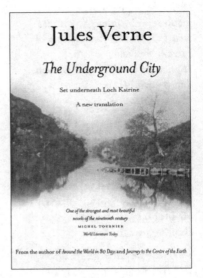

Jules Verne

The Underground City

Set underneath Loch Katrine

A new translation

One of the strangest and most beautiful novels of the nineteenth century
MICHEL TOURNIER
World Literature Today

From the author of *Around the World in 80 Days* and *Journey to the Centre of the Earth*

One of the strangest and most beautiful novels of the 19th century.
Michel Tournier,
WORLD LITERATURE TODAY

The Green Ray

Jules Verne

Translated by Karen Loukes, with an afterword by Professor Ian Thompson

ISBN 978 1905222 12 4 PBK £7.99

The green ray – a beam of green light seen at the horizon at the setting of the sun – is a phenomenon that is well known to sailors, who are often able to see it over the edge of the ocean. When a newspaper article tells Helena Campbell, whose impending arranged marriage is less than a love match, that seeing the green ray is an indication of true love, she refuses to marry anyone until she has seen it. Her quest to view the green ray takes her on an island-hopping tour of the Hebrides that nearly costs her her life, and Helena must ask herself – is seeing the green ray worth it? With which of her suitors will Helena see the ray? Will she ever see it at all?

The Green Ray has all the hallmarks of a Verne classic –

danger, romance and of course a tale of marvellous adventure. This new translation of Jules Verne's 'lost' Scottish novel recaptures the spirit of the original French text.

Details of these and other books published by Luath Press can be found at:
www.luath.co.uk

Luath Press Limited
committed to publishing well written books worth reading

LUATH PRESS takes its name from Robert Burns, whose little collie Luath (*Gael.*, swift or nimble) tripped up Jean Armour at a wedding and gave him the chance to speak to the woman who was to be his wife and the abiding love of his life. Burns called one of 'The Twa Dogs' Luath after Cuchullin's hunting dog in Ossian's *Fingal*. Luath Press was established in 1981 in the heart of Burns country, and is now based a few steps up the road from Burns' first lodgings on Edinburgh's Royal Mile.
Luath offers you distinctive writing with a hint of unexpected pleasures.

Most bookshops in the UK, the US, Canada, Australia, New Zealand and parts of Europe either carry our books in stock or can order them for you. To order direct from us, please send a £sterling cheque, postal order, international money order or your credit card details (number, address of cardholder and expiry date) to us at the address below. Please add post and packing as follows: UK – £1.00 per delivery address; overseas surface mail – £2.50 per delivery address; overseas airmail – £3.50 for the first book to each delivery address, plus £1.00 for each additional book by airmail to the same address. If your order is a gift, we will happily enclose your card or message at no extra charge.

Luath Press Limited
543/2 Castlehill
The Royal Mile
Edinburgh EH1 2ND
Scotland
Telephone: 0131 225 4326 (24 hours)
Fax: 0131 225 4324
email: sales@luath.co.uk
Website: www.luath.co.uk